Influencing Attitudes
and Changing Behavior

A Basic Introduction to Relevant Methodology, Theory, and Applications

PHILIP ZIMBARDO
and
EBBE B. EBBESEN
Stanford University
In collaboration with Christina Maslach

REVISED PRINTING

ADDISON-WESLEY PUBLISHING COMPANY
Reading, Massachusetts
Menlo Park, California · *London* · *Don Mills, Ontario*

TOPICS IN SOCIAL PSYCHOLOGY

Charles A. Kiesler, University of Kansas, Series Editor

Revised printing, July 1970

ISBN 0-201-08790-1
GHIJKLMNOP-CO-787654

Foreword

It is becoming increasingly difficult for anyone to be a generalist in social psychology. Not only is the number of articles published zooming, but new researchable areas of interest are multiplying as well. A researcher finds more fascinating topics these days than he used to, but he also finds himself behind in his reading of all but one or two of them. As a result, the quality of the broad introductory book in social psychology has suffered. No one can any longer be an expert in all of social psychology.

As an alternative, we offer the present series, *Topics in Social Psychology,* directed toward the student with no prior background in social psychology. Taken as a whole, the series adequately covers the field of social psychology, but it has the advantage that each short book was written by an expert in the area. The given instructor can select some subset of the books to make up his course, the particular subset depending upon his biases and inclinations. In addition, the individual volumes could be useful in several ways: as supplementary reading in, perhaps, a sociology course; to introduce more advanced courses (for example, a graduate seminar in attitude change); or just for peeking at recent developments in social psychology.

This volume covers the area of attitude change, which to my mind forms the central core of social psychology. Zimbardo (collaborating with Ebbesen) approaches the topics in a style we have come to expect of him, fresh and inventive.

Charles A. Kiesler

Preface

Most texts on attitude change are disappointing to the nonprofessional reader, and most courses devoted to this topic are uninspiring (even with competent instruction). Two apparent reasons for this sorry state of affairs center on the nature of modern social psychology and the complexity of the problems investigated. Researchers in this area are not concerned with changing attitudes, but with using the attitude change paradigm to study basic psychological processes and the operation of theoretically relevant variables. While such a scientific approach is necessary to advance knowledge, it often loses sight of the end product of the search—the manipulation and control of attitudes and related behaviors. In addition, there is a discrepancy between what students expect from their study of this area and what they learn, because the complex problems and issues studied have not resulted in a nice, neat bundle of conclusions. Rather, there is much controversy over inconsistent findings and inadequate theory, with answers being sought in subtle nuances of experimental methodology. The lack of standardization of basic definitions and operations, as well as a simplistic reliance on paper-and-pencil measures of attitude, makes this an unrewarding area of study for the student.

We hope to offset this negative trend by using a scientifically unorthodox approach, namely a practical, problem-centered focus. What are the problems facing all of us which demand that we know how to induce change in others or to resist attempts to change us? What are the questions we must ask, to orient ourselves, before seriously embarking on a program to change the attitudes of other people? Where do we look for answers? What can we learn from the humanities, practical arts (law, politics), and social science? What findings do social psychologists offer which may be useful in building a technology of attitude change? Where do such findings come from? What are the features of an experiment? What is unique about an attitude change experiment? What do representative experiments actually look like? Can we increase our confidence in the results of experiments by learning to evaluate research critically? What help can theory offer in guiding our search for relevant knowledge and in making sense out of what we know? In this book we consider each of these questions in some detail. Once the reader is armed with critical appreciation of experimental methodology and theory, and knows where to look for answers and what he is likely to find there, we finally consider several practical problems as they have been studied in real life situations: psychological warfare, prejudice, police interrogation, consumer motivation, and supersalesmanship.

Our goal in all this is twofold: to turn the reader on to the potential value and excitement inherent in the study of attitude change, and to provide the serious student with a primer which may be an impetus to further academic study. To achieve both of these desired outcomes, we have at times been very general in our approach and assumed a reader with little or no relevant background. At other times, however, we have gone into considerable detail on points which would be of interest primarily to psychologically or sociologically oriented students. We have in this brief introduction to attitude change suggested little more than an approach; the reader is referred to other texts by our colleagues for a more thorough survey of theories, findings, and issues (cf. books by Hovland, Janis and Kelley; Cohen; Insko; Kiesler, Collins and Miller; and Greenwald, Brock, and Ostrom). We have not identified the name of each researcher with every finding presented because such information is of little value to the general reader. Teachers using this book as a text can provide such information, fill out the skeleton we have presented of methodology and theory, and suggest applications to problems of relevance to their students.

In conclusion, we would like to express our thanks to the following copyright holders for giving us permission to use quotations or figures from their publications: American Psychological Association; Doubleday & Company, Inc.; William Heinemann, Ltd.; Houghton Mifflin Company; Hutchinson Publishing Group, Ltd.; McGraw Hill Book Company; Princeton University Press; Rand McNally & Company; Random House, Inc.; Charles C Thomas, Publisher; Herbert I. Abelson; Marvin Karlins; and Springer Publishing Company, Inc. Also, we want to express our special thanks to Mrs. Judy Fukuda for her help in typing the manuscript.

Stanford, California   P. Z.
February 1969   E.B.E.

Contents

CHAPTER ONE

Posing Problems in
Attitude and Behavior Modification

"The concept of attitudes is probably the most distinctive and indispensable concept in contemporary American social psychology."

Gordon Allport

In thirty-seven years the world population will be twice as large as it is now. At such a rate of growth, in 900 years there would be 6,000,000,000,000,000 people on the earth. If six million billion people were on the earth, then, laying people end to end, there would be a mass of human beings 100 deep over every surface—land, sea, and ice—of the earth. Of course, such a high population doubling rate would not, and could not, occur. Human beings would begin to die faster than they were reproducing, many years before so many people populated the earth.

The reader has heard about the overpopulation problem before, and may feel that "science" will someday solve the problem. Let us look at a few specific examples and see what the problems are that face "science."

In Indonesia, the population doubling rate is thirty-one years. This means that if the Indonesian people were willing, which they probably are not, merely to maintain their present very low standard of living, they would have to double their food production every thirty-one years to feed the added population. But that means using more land for food. However, since even the land in the United States tends to lose its food-producing capacity at about the rate of one percent a year, *more* than double the land space would be needed to merely double the food production. But the bigger the population, the more land space the population needs on which to live. Using more land for food, and doubling the number of people means that less than one quarter of the present land space would be available for living in only thirty-one years. But if "science" could come up with some way to feed double the present number of people in thirty-one years, what about sixty-two years from now, when the reader's children are looking for food? "Science" has to double food production again or, in comparison to what it is now, quadruple it.

The chances are that the physical "sciences," as good as they have been, will not be able to help us nearly as much as would be required. There is only so much land space on the earth. Moving enough people from the earth to another planet is almost impossible. In order to keep up with the present population doubling rate, approximately four billion people would have to be transported to other planets every thirty-seven years. This means that every day, assuming we could build rocket ships to transport 100 people per rocket, we would have to send off 2000 rockets.

This review of the problems facing a physical "science" solution to overpopulation suggests that solutions should also be sought elsewhere, namely, in the social sciences. If people would practice some form of birth control, overpopulation could be completely prevented. How can the social sciences begin to get all the people on earth to practice birth control? What are some of the problems in this approach?

One barrier to birth control is governmental policies. The former president of Indonesia, Sukarno, believed that the only way in which the country could achieve world power was by increasing its population. This belief was instituted as a national policy, so that high birth rates were rewarded with praise from government officials. In addition, the government requested that the bare-breasted Balinese dancers try to sexually arouse their male audiences so that men would want to have sexual intercourse more often. Statues and monuments were raised all over the country in honor of sex and reproduction. Not surprisingly, the male population soon began doing exactly what President Sukarno had hoped they would. Now, however, the present Indonesian government has come to realize the dangers of overpopulation toward which the country is heading and has decided to reverse the whole process. They no longer want the dancers to perform bare-breasted, and are trying to institute a program of monogamy and birth control. However, religious beliefs can also discourage birth control. A large percentage of the Indonesian population is either Moslem or Catholic. The problem is, how does the government induce Moslems to have only one wife and, in addition, practice birth control? How can it change the attitudes of Catholics towards birth control?

There is another, deeply ingrained attitude which runs counter to acceptance of birth control devices—the romantic attitude of "the spontaneous sexual encounter," without premeditation or preparation. This may have to be the major target of any attitude change approach in many cultures (along with the embarrassment felt by the youth in purchasing birth control devices). A recent survey of sexual behavior at Stanford University (Rowland and Young, 1968) revealed the remarkable fact that of the 40 co-eds interviewed who had engaged in sexual intercourse 70 percent reported that no birth control devices were used during their first act of intercourse. For males, the figure was a comparable 66 percent (of 53 students). What is more surprising is that half of all the girls and more than half of all the males who had subsequent sexual intercourse did not use birth control regularly. However, approximately 85 percent of both the males and females who had not yet had intercourse reported that they *planned* to use birth control devices. It seems obvious that although students believed birth control was a "good thing," their use of such devices when faced with the "real nitty gritty" situation was far from that indicated by such a belief. Thus, the problem is not limited to persuading unintelligent natives in the so-called underdeveloped countries; there are powerful forces of resistance to combat even among the most intelligent and "sexually liberated" males and females.

What if you, the reader, were hired to change people's attitudes toward birth control? What would you do to induce attitude change so that famine and unnecessary human deaths were prevented? What information would you draw on to help you decide what techniques to use to produce attitude change? In light of questions like these, the problem of how to produce attitude change and what techniques are most effective becomes most interesting.

The attitude change process cannot be ignored, since it is so much a part of every human being's life. Every day, each of us tries to influence someone's attitudes or is influenced by someone else's attempt to change our attitudes. What can be done to increase the likelihood that people whose attitudes you are trying to change will actually be influenced? This is the main question which this book attempts to answer.

Most books on attitude change are written from a formal, sterile, scientific point of view. Typically, they merely outline either theories or experiments on attitude change. The approach of this book will be a bit different. Throughout the entire book we will be asking you to put yourself into a specific situation and think how you would go about solving some practical problems involving attitude change. For example, we will ask such questions as, where would you look for methods or techniques to produce attitude change? How would you know you had produced the change you had hoped to produce? Is it change in existing attitudes or the formation of new attitudes which is required? What do you mean by attitudes in the first place?

PRACTICAL PROBLEMS FOR YOU TO SOLVE

Let us assume that you are being hired to design a program for solving problems, such as promoting birth control, or any of the problems to be described. You should be asking questions about what needs to be done, what facilities are available, what characteristics of the people being changed would be worth knowing, etc. For example, suppose that a fraternity whose recruiting had fallen off in the past few years hired you to increase the number of freshmen joining that fraternity. What questions would you want answered? You might first want to know if the fraternity merely wanted to increase the number of freshmen joining or whether it was also important to change the image of the fraternity for nonfraternity members as well. Does the fraternity want to be seen as a swinging, yet intellectual house, in addition to increasing recruitment? It would be important to know how long the fraternity wanted the increase in recruitment to last. How enduring a change is required? Changes which are meant to last over long periods of time would probably be more expensive and difficult to produce. As a behavioral engineer, hired to produce changes in the behavior and attitudes of freshmen, the questions you might want answered before you set your change program in motion would be numerous.

What about a problem involving prejudice? Wouldn't you first want to know with what kind of prejudice you had to deal? For example, if you were hired by a minority group to change some majority group's prejudiced attitudes towards them, would the techniques required to produce such attitude change be different from those required to change young black children's prejudiced attitudes toward themselves? In the first case, too much change would certainly not be a major problem. On the other hand, hard-sell training in black power could result in an overreaction in which black children reject all information from whites, even when it might be valuable to them. Thus, being able to control the amount of attitude change is highly important since you don't want to create new problems while solving the old.

A problem more relevant to the business world might be the tobacco industry's interest in changing the public's attitude toward smoking. If you were hired to work on this problem, one question you would certainly want answered is, what sort of approach would be most effective? Should you merely attack the suggested link between smoking and lung cancer, or would better results be produced if your emphasis was on increasing the attractiveness of smoking, in spite of its negative effects? Again, you might want to know what is important to the particular cigarette company—sales, or image, or both?

One problem faced by the Army is how to train people to shoot guns at the enemy. Would it be better for the Army to develop aggressive attitudes in their men so that they enjoy killing, or merely to teach them to fire at the enemy when in battle? What would you do if hired by a group of new inductees who wanted you to help them resist either of these attempts by the Army?

Along a different line, suppose you were hired by a group of college freshmen to change girls' attitudes toward pre-marital sexual relations. One of the first questions you might ask is how general the change is supposed to be. Should the girls only change their attitudes toward sexual relations for one guy, or for all guys, or what? Alternatively, suppose you were hired by these same girls' mothers to set up a program to ensure that the girls resisted the previously mentioned influence attempt. What would you want to know from the mothers? What techniques would you use to increase the resistance of these girls? Obviously, one question that arises when considering change programs like these is the extent to which you are intimately involved in the topic of the change program. Surely girls would react differently than boys to either of these last two job offers.

QUESTIONS TO ASK

Some of these problems suggest that it may be possible to make up sets of questions concerning the attitude change which is required. One set has to do with the nature of the change itself.

1.   How specific does the change need to be? In the pre-marital sex example, is it just one's attitudes toward pre-marital sex with some particular person that are being changed, or one's attitudes toward sex in general?

2.   How long does the change have to last?

3.   How many people have to be changed—one, some, or many?

4.   What is to be changed—how people think, how they talk, or how they behave nonverbally? Is it enough to produce unconscious change, or must the people be aware that they are changing?

5.   Is change of some particular behavior or attitude required, or must a whole new set of behaviors or attitudes be created?

Another set of questions deals with the control over the situation which you, as a hired consultant, would have.

1.   Do you control all the communication media?

2.   If you do control the media, is it likely that people will listen?

3.   Are there other agents trying to produce change in the opposite direction from you who are also competing for the attention of your audience?

4.   What are the time limits you have?

5.   How much money, resources, etc. are available?

6.   How will *you*, personally, be presented to the people whose attitudes or behavior you are trying to change? Will you be seen as an agent trying to produce change, or will you be seen as someone just interested in the problem?

7.   Will you have control over the people who are available for change, or will they volunteer or select themselves?

From an entirely different point of view, another set of questions you would surely want to consider deals with the consequences to *you* of accepting or not accepting the job.

1.   Will you be required to have future interactions with the people you are trying to change? Will they get to know you as some obnoxious person who is always trying to influence them?

2.   What is "your stake" in the problem topic? Are you biased on that topic? Are you committed to one side already?

3.   What about the consequences of being a successful manipulator? Will you be seen, and will you see yourself, as a Hitler or Goebbels?

4.   How would you react to failure?

5.   Might you, yourself, be changed by applying your own techniques?

The remaining sets of questions which you might want to ask deal with the actual techniques of change that could be used, where to find and how to evaluate different techniques, and finally, how to apply these techniques of change to real problem areas. These are the main questions for which this book will attempt to provide some answers.

WHAT ARE ATTITUDES, ANYWAY?

In order to provide answers to questions about the most effective techniques of attitude change, it is obvious that we first need to know the kinds of problem areas to which the techniques of attitude and behavior change are applicable. Rather than supply the reader with what may be a biased and limited list of problems, it would seem more reasonable to let the reader devise his own. Therefore, let us consider how attitudes and attitude change have traditionally been conceptualized so that the reader can begin thinking about the problems to which he might want to apply these techniques.

Attitudes have generally been regarded as either mental readinesses or implicit predispositions which exert some general and consistent influence on a fairly large class of evaluative responses. These responses are usually directed toward some object, person, or group. In addition, attitudes are seen as enduring predispositions, but ones which are *learned* rather than innate. Thus, even though attitudes are *not* momentarily transient, they are susceptible to change.

What are the crucial components of this conceptualization of attitudes, and how are these components relevant to any practical problem? Thinking of attitudes as underlying learned predispositions suggests that all the techniques which are known to increase or decrease learning should be applicable to producing change in attitudes. Rewards and punishments should be highly effective means of producing attitude change, and it should be possible to use them to predict the amount of generalized attitude change that will occur. In essence, all the techniques relevant to learning any materials should be relevant to learning and changing attitudes.

A practical consequence which follows from conceptualizing attitudes as enduring rather than momentary states is that by changing people's underlying attitudes, it should be possible to produce longlasting rather than transient changes in behavior. For example, in Indonesia it would not be enough to have the population practice birth control for one month. What is required is a change lasting over many *generations*. It is assumed that by making people's underlying *attitudes* toward birth control very positive, birth control would be practiced for a much longer time. Hopefully, this positive attitude would be more likely to be transmitted from those directly influenced by the change program to subsequent generations than if only the overt behavior of using birth control devices was changed. Thus, by changing underlying attitudes, more enduring changes in behavior should be produced than by trying to directly change only the behavior in question.

A practical consequence of thinking about attitudes as highly generalized predispositions is that by changing attitudes, one should also be able to produce *many* specific changes in overt behavior. For example, in trying to produce changes in black children's self-conceptions, it is not sufficient to merely get these children to *say* they think more highly of themselves as black people, but rather the goal is to have the children behave towards themselves, towards other blacks, and towards other whites in a host of changed ways. An efficient method for changing many specific behaviors at once would be to change one or two underlying general dispositions or attitudes.

We have seen how the traditional view of attitudes as enduring, generalized, learned predispositions suggests a number of practical implications which could be important. However, the utility of thinking about attitudes in this way is not only a function of these possible practical implications. A more important consideration is the extent to which the traditional view suggests how attitudes are related to other psychological processes, how attitudes are formed, how they are measured, and how they are manipulated. Merely defining attitudes as enduring, general, and learned tells us little about how to measure or change them. In fact, defining attitudes in this way only implies that they are states which exist inside the person and which exert some control over his overt behavior. How they exert control is left ambiguous. Therefore, to solve these problems, attitudes have generally been divided into three components: affect, cognition, and behavior. The affective component consists of a person's evaluation of, liking of, or emotional response to some object or person. The cognitive component has been conceptualized as a person's beliefs about, or factual knowledge of, the object or person. The behavioral component involves the person's overt behavior directed toward the object or person. If attitudes are conceptualized in this way, we can see how techniques designed to change only a person's emotional reactions toward some object or person would be attacking only one component of the attitude in question. Not only does this component conception of attitude suggest interesting methods of changing attitudes, but it also provides us with ideas about how to measure them.[1] The affective component could be measured by physiological responses or verbal statements of like and dislike, while the cognitive component might be measured by self-ratings of beliefs or by the amount of knowledge which a person has about some topic. The behavioral component could be measured by direct observation of how the person behaves in specific stimulus situations.

If the reader were hired to change certain attitudes, what would he need, besides the traditional conceptualizations of attitude, to develop an effective change program? The remainder of the book is designed to present the reader with some information which could help him answer this question.

---

[1] The reader is referred to Postscript *A* for a more detailed analysis of attitude measurement.

CHAPTER TWO

Considering Where to Look for Answers, and What We Know from Social Psychological Studies

Assume that you have agreed to accept the challenge of trying to develop a program to change attitudes relevant to one of the problems depicted in the first chapter. Assume further that you have asked the kind of questions we outlined there, in order to get a general orientation as to: the nature of the change desired (e.g., immediate or delayed, specific or general, temporary or enduring, attitudinal or behavioral); the kind of target population (single individual, small groups, institution, or nation); characteristics of the recipients of the influence attempt (intelligence, education, sex, social class, value structure, etc.); media available to you in the situation; and presence of counter-information and opposition influence.

Once armed with the answers to questions like these, you are in a position to begin drawing your blueprint for attitude modification. In order to proceed you need to know the resources at your disposal (money, assistants, degree of control possible, and local contacts), time limits, and the constraints peculiar to the situation in which you will establish your program. It is also necessary to be aware of legal, moral, and ethical considerations.

Now what? Even with all this information, you still can not begin until you have a grasp of techniques for producing change, important variables in the process, general principles of attitude change, and methods for evaluating the change to determine if your program works. Finally, in your approach you will want to avoid the pitfalls, errors, and artifacts of other investigators. (An artifact occurs when a researcher believes that a change was produced by factor A when, in fact, that change was really produced by factor B.) This chapter provides some guidelines as to where your search for relevant information might start and also offers a capsule summary of attitude change variables, techniques, and processes.

WHERE TO LOOK FOR IDEAS

The attempt by one person to change the attitudes and behavior of others is an historically ageless one and a basic part of Western tradition. The story of Satan's temptation of Eve and her subsequent persuasion of Adam recurs in many forms in our literary heritage. It may be profitable to start a search for sources of possible relevance to our goal by turning to history, literature, and religion before examining what we can extract from the disciplines of behavioral science, especially anthropology, sociology, and psychology. Obviously, in a brief introductory text like the present one, all we can do is suggest that such sources are worth your consideration, and then briefly document why. We offer as an interesting exercise for students of history and literature the task of searching primary source material in their own fields with an eye toward systematically organizing and categorizing it in terms germane to the process of interpersonal influence.

History

For our present purpose it may be instructive to see what we can learn from two former masters of the persuasion process, Niccolo Machiavelli and Adolf Hitler.

Machiavelli

Communicator characteristics

... nothing is so apt to restrain an excited multitude as the reverence inspired by some grave and dignified man of authority who opposes them ... therefore whoever is at the head of an army, or whoever happens to be a magistrate in a city where sedition lies broken out, should present himself before the multitude with all possible grace and dignity, and attired with all the insignia of his rank, so as to inspire the more respect. (*Discourses,* p. 251)

Disguised intent of persuader

For he who for a time has seemed good, and for purposes of his own wants to become bad, should do it gradually, and should seem to be brought to it by the force of circumstances; so that, before his changed nature deprives him of his former friends, he may have gained new ones, and that his authority may not be diminished by the change. Otherwise his deception will be discovered, and he will lose his friends and be ruined. (*Discourses*, p. 225)

The use of prestige effects

In truth, there never was any remarkable lawgiver amongst any people who did not resort to divine authority, as otherwise his laws would not have been accepted by the people; for there are many good laws, the importance of which is known to the sagacious lawgiver, but the reasons for which are not sufficiently evident to enable him to persuade others to submit to them; and therefore do wise men, for the purpose of removing this difficulty, resort to divine authority. (*Discourses*, p. 147)

Hitler

Tailoring the message to the audience

The receptive ability of the masses is very limited, their understanding small; on the other hand, they have a great power of forgetting. This being so, all effective propaganda must be confined to a very few points which must be brought out in the form of slogans until the very last man is enabled to comprehend what is meant by any slogan. If this principle is sacrificed to the desire to be many-sided, it will dissipate the effectual working of the propaganda, for the people will be unable to digest or retain the material that is offered them. It will, moreover, weaken and finally cancel its own effectiveness. (*Mein Kampf*, p. 77)

The basis for emotional appeals

An immense majority of the people are so feminine in nature and point of view that their thoughts and actions are governed more by feeling and sentiment than by reasoned consideration. This sentiment is, however, not complicated, but very simple and consistent. It does not differentiate much, but it is either positive or negative, love or hate, truth or lies, never half one and half the other, and so on. (*Mein Kampf*, p. 78)

Qualter, in his treatise *Propaganda and Psychological Warfare* (1962), describes further how Hitler devised a systematic program to effectively change the attitudes and values of an entire nation, a program in which every detail was turned to the advantage of the propagandist.

Uniforms, bands, flags, symbols were all part of the German propaganda machine, designed by Hitler and Goebbels to increase the impact of strong words by evidence of strong deeds. Meetings were not just occasions for people to make speeches, they were carefully planned theatrical productions in which settings, lighting, background music, and the timing of entrances and exits were devised to maximize the emotional fervor of an audience already brought to fever pitch by an hour or more given over to singing and the shouting of slogans . . . (p.112)

Literature

From literature, one can derive ideas for many potentially testable hypotheses about the dynamics of social influence processes.

Marc Antony's classic funeral oration in Shakespeare's *Julius Caesar* is the best example of an explicit attempt to persuade an audience to alter its attitudes and modify its behavior. From an analysis of the techniques ascribed to Antony we may abstract several hypotheses about attitude change, one of which has been experimentally validated. The reader will recall the situation facing Antony and the goal of his persuasive communication. Cassius and the conspirators had convinced Brutus to join them in killing Caesar in order to use Brutus' good reputation with the citizens to their advantage. At Caesar's funeral, Brutus, speaking first, justifies the assassination as a necessary act, done not from ambition or hatred, not from loving Caesar less, but from loving Rome more. The audience is swayed by his argument, and is set to oppose Marc Antony, whom they expect will give a pro-Caesar or anti-Brutus speech.

Antony purposely chooses to be the last speaker and begins with introductory remarks which confound the expectations of the crowd by affirming his essential agreement with their position. He has not come to praise Caesar; his function is merely to bury him. He, like the crowd, must acknowledge that Brutus is an honorable man. Having created this intellectual basis for common agreement with the crowd, he then effectively proceeds by indirection and emotional appeals to force them to draw the conclusion that Caesar was unjustly murdered and that Brutus and the other murderers should be driven out.

There are many techniques illustrated in Marc Antony's speech, but one deserves special attention because it was used in a real life situation. T. N. Ewing, a psychologist, in 1942 validated the principle that when presenting a persuasive communication whose conclusion is in disagreement with the audience, the audience will be more influenced if the communicator first agrees with the audience's initial position. A speech which argued against the Ford production line was presented to an audience which was initially pro-Ford. It was more influential in producing anti-Ford attitudes in a group where the speaker began by defining himself as pro-Ford than in a group given the identical speech without the Marc Antony-type of introductory statement.

Religion

The reader might also find fruitful, in his search for techniques of attitude change, accounts of how religious evangelists operate. We can see how skillfully the great mass revivalists like Billy Sunday, Oral Roberts, Prophet

Jones, and Billy Graham used approaches in which guilt and fear were aroused. Then, by providing an opportunity for emotional catharsis and well-timed reassurance, the audience is directed away from a life of self-indulgence and sin toward one of self-sacrifice in God's name. Most significant is their use of public commitment—of coming forward, taking a vow, making an overt pledge, or speaking out. They do not wait until their audience believes before requesting it to act, but rather work on the now firmly established psychological principle (to be elaborated in Chapter 5) that beliefs change following a commitment to behavior discrepant with the original beliefs. In fact, in the Old Testament the rabbis are enjoined not to make their parishioners or converts believe in God *before* they are asked to pray, but to have them pray first so that belief will follow.

Law

Trial lawyers have offered us dramatic descriptions of the myriad factors and seemingly trivial details to which they must be responsive in order to persuade a jury of twelve individuals to agree with their conclusion and reject that of their opponents. Louis Nizer's *My Life in Court* (1961) offers us much of value with reference to significant audience characteristics (such as sex, ethnic group, and social class) which must be taken into account in planning any communication strategy. He offers hunches about how to "size up" your audience (here, the jury), and how to assess their values and attitudes, and he suggests approaches which appeal to and exploit points of vulnerability. The following are some selected tactics used by Nizer:

Order of presentation of arguments

1) But if the attorney stays within his capacity to perform, the opening statement can be an invaluable forensic weapon. By a skillful presentation of what he intends to prove, set opposite the issues in the case, he can convert a mere informative exercise into a persuasive plea. Of course he should not tell all. Indeed, he may even spread some leaves over the traps, so that his adversary will tread more readily over them. But the opportunity to condition the jury favorably is as limitless as the attorney's art. (p.42)

2) The plaintiff has a decided advantage in summing up last. He can analyze the argument just heard by the jury and point out the facts it omitted and the omissions in proof it assumed existed. (p.432)

Resistance to persuasion

When I am required to sum up first, I endeavor to prepare the jury so that it will not yield to the blandishments of my adversary. I remind the jury that he will have the last word and that I will not be permitted to reply. I tell them that I must depend on their recollections to correct any misstatement of fact which my opponent, who follows me, may make. I must rely on their discriminating judgment to reject any false arguments. Then, as I proceed to build my own case, I anticipate the contentions of my adversary. I announce his slogans and attempt to destroy them, asking the jurors to become my watchmen when they hear such sophistry, and reject it as an insult to their intelligence. (p.434)

Eye contact

It is an early opportunity to look each juror in the eye and by sincerity and earnestness make contact with him. It is interesting to observe the bland look on a juror's face when you begin, perhaps even a cynical smile, and how he is caught up in the drama of your recital, his face responding properly with varying emotions of sympathy or resentment as the arguments make inroads upon him. Finally, when you walk up and back, and his eyes follow and are riveted upon you, the persuasive effort has begun successfully. (p.42)

Anthropology

In New Guinea, some aboriginal tribes still use stone axes in preference to more efficient and durable metal axes. This cultural lag in getting people to adopt new techniques proven superior to traditional ones is fostered by a general resistance against giving up old ways of responding. From anthropological studies of this phenomenon across different cultures we may be able to come up with some general description of the conditions which maintain this resistance and of techniques to weaken or eliminate it. Before you could begin to develop a program for changing attitudes toward birth control in Indonesia, for example, you would have to become acquainted with culture-bound ways of perceiving and reacting. Certain attitudes and values are often so widely accepted in a given culture that they are virtually truisms for all members of that culture, and rarely, if ever, are contrary points of view presented. Likewise, an investigator may filter his observations through glass ground by biases in his own culture. In this way, he may be unaware of, or misperceive, variables and processes which may be important for his understanding of why people hold the attitudes they do, and how best to change them. Within our own culture, this is the charge levelled against white middle-class reformers trying to produce change in lower-class black ghettos.

SOCIOLOGY AND PSYCHOLOGY

This brief survey of where to look for useful background information and ideas now focuses on the two disciplines in social science which have the most obvious and direct relevance to our general problem: sociology and psychology. Although at some points of intersection it is difficult to tell if a given piece of research belongs to one or the other of these areas, there are several critical differences which hold for most comparisons between the two. The sociologist interested in influence and persuasion would direct his attention to processes existing in society, in institutions, and within groups, while the psychologist's unit of study is the individual organism. For example, the way in which assembly-line production and urbanization create feelings of alienation in a society is the sociological analogy of the psychological study of individual feelings of rejection and self-esteem. The two differ, then, in the unit of analysis, the variables and processes studied (intraindividual or intergroup), and in techniques of investigation.

They are both on the scientific end of a continuum, the other end of which is represented by literature, humanistic studies, and arts. Thus they both propose formal techniques for gathering evidence which allow objective conclusions to be drawn independently of the personal biases of the investigator. They rely upon controlled observation as a major method in collecting information about behavior, and hold their procedures and results up for public scrutiny, critical evaluation, and reproducibility.

Sociological research usually attempts to uncover things as they exist, and therefore relies upon observations in naturally existing settings. Some psychological research, however, attempts to abstract the causal elements from complex phenomena. This is best achieved by a conceptual analysis, and then by the validation of this reasoning in experiments which represent the "pure" functioning of the relevant variables uncontaminated by the many other things going on in the natural situation.

In the next chapter we will describe what is unique about experiments dealing with attitude change. (In postscript B we will discuss what an experiment is.) But first we have to make a few more distinctions, describe schema for organizing what psychologists know about persuasion, and then outline what it is they claim to know about changing attitudes.

Social Psychology

It is primarily the sub-area of social psychology, within the broader discipline of psychology, which studies attitude change. Social psychologists study individual behavior as it is influenced by the operation of social stimuli, those generated by the existence of other people. But a social psychologist might also study social behavior in response to structural stimuli which are not obviously "social" in themselves.

Social psychological investigators have carved up their subject matter in different ways, adopted different orientations, and concentrated their attention upon different processes. This specialization, on the one hand, has resulted in more intensive analysis of selected phenomena, but on the other hand it means that researchers may use different labels to refer to a common body of evidence and that similarities tend to be obscured by emphasis on differences.

Thus our reader, when opening a text in social psychology, would be directed to a special section devoted to "Communication and Attitude Change." A separate section might deal with "Person Perception" (development of attitudes toward people in general) or "Prejudice" (a specific set of evaluative attitudes toward people) or "Conformity" and "Group Dynamics." In each of these, the behavior studied is often changes in attitude, or behavior presumably based upon related attitudes.

Your search for relevant information will therefore have to take account of this peculiarity; namely, that the basis for organization of materials is not necessarily in terms of the behavior studied, but according to a more general psychological process, or to arbitrary labelling schemes. For example, a study showing that group discussion and commitment were more effective than a lecture in getting housewives during World War II to agree to serve their families available but undesirable glandular meats (Lewin, Lippitt, and White, 1939) is not listed as a study in attitude change but as one in group dynamics.

The formal attitude change approach. The school of Communication and Attitude Change (exemplified by Carl Hovland and his associates at Yale University) differs from that of Group Dynamics (exemplified by Kurt Lewin and the research from the Center for Group Dynamics at the University of Michigan) in several basic assumptions. The Yale approach is derived from a learning theory orientation and assumes that man is a rational, information-processing organism who can be motivated to attend to a communication, to learn its contents, and to incorporate them into his verbal repertoire of responses when this learning is rewarded. Thus the instrument of change is a formal, structured communication. The agent of change is either the actual or anticipated reward for agreeing with the communicator, or else the awareness of the logical and rational necessity for accepting the information and position advanced.

The group dynamics approach. In contrast, the Group Dynamics approach is derived from a cognitive, field-theory orientation, and assumes that man is a social being who needs other people as a basis for (a) self-knowledge, (b) determining appropriate responses to environmental demands, and (c) channeling and regulating his current behavior through the operation of group norms. The instrument of change is a group norm discrepant with the individual's attitude or behavior, a norm which may be communicated *informally.* The agent of change is pressure toward uniformity within a group, coupled with a need to be accepted in the group, or a fear of being rejected from it.

Since another book in this series (by Kiesler and Kiesler) deals exclusively with the topic of conformity and group processes, we can now focus on social psychological research which applies directly to designing a program of attitude change.

VARIABLES IN THE ATTITUDE CHANGE PROCESS

One descriptive schema for categorizing the many known variables in attitude change characterizes the essential sequence as, "Who says what to whom and with what effect." Such an approach leads to an organization of our knowledge under the headings of: communicator or source; communication or message; audience, recipients, or target population; and response dimensions. Not included in this paradigm, but clearly relevant, are the media of transmission of the message and the situation in which the message is received.

Source. Aristotle noted that an effective communicator must be a man of good sense, good will, and good moral character. Therefore it is not surprising that the major *communicator* variables which have been systematically studied are those dealing with his credibility, specifically expertise and trustworthiness. How much knowledge and background does he have pertinent to the topic, and what are his motives for personal gain in advocating a particular position? Also studied have been general traits which are irrelevant to the specific issue communicated, e.g., the race of the communicator, or the effect of his personal behavior on the recipients. We should mention in passing that, in scientific research in speech and communications, source credibility is studied under the heading of "ethos." Ethos attributes found to be important (by means of a mathematical technique called factor analysis), in addition to the communicator's expertness and good intentions, are: dynamism, sociability, authoritative manner, reliability, and personal attractiveness. (See Anderson and Clevenger, 1963, and Griffin, 1967.) Many other variables *ought* to increase the effectiveness of the source, such as his social status, age, physical appearance, and speaking style, but these have not been studied experimentally.

Communication. Some communication variables which have been studied are: (a) the order of presentation of the arguments: should the strongest arguments come last ("climax order") or first ("anticlimax")? (b) primacy-recency effectiveness: in a two-sided debate should you present your case first or last? (c) one-sided or two-sided presentation: should you present only your position, or your opponent's as well, and then refute it? (d) explicit or implicit conclusion drawing: should the communicator draw the conclusion explicitly or allow the audience to do so from the arguments presented? (e) content characteristics: rational or emotional appeals, fear-stimulating properties, verb forms and other linguistic aspects.

Audience. Audience characteristics which have received serious attention in recent studies are termed "persuasibility factors." They include the ability to understand the message (primarily intelligence), personality traits relevant to acceptance of the message (primarily self-esteem, dogmatism, and

authoritarianism), and general motivational traits (such as anxiety and involvement).

Other, clearly more important audience variables are those which are
not attributes, but rather consequences of reacting to the communication
situation in a particular way: active participation in presenting the message
versus passive exposure to it, commitment to a position, perception of
choice ("reactance" to limits on one's freedom), the number and quality of
justifications one has for adopting a given behavior, effort involved in making a response, and the opportunity to rehearse counter-arguments. Other
"organismic" variables which affect persuasibility are the person's information level, "cognitive structure" (system of beliefs and their degree of
organization), the motivational basis for his initial attitude, the relation of
the proposed attitude to his more general value structure, and his critical-
evaluative ability. Another variable which is crucial in estimating the probability that a specified persuasive communication will succeed in changing
attitudes is the extremity of the initial position that the person has
taken.

The schema we have just described is a static, atheoretical, purely
descriptive classification model. A quite different formulation for helping us
to think in a coherent way about the attitude change sequence describes
some of the primary psychological *processes* involved. It has the virtue of
leading us to think of how variables interact or operate differently at different stages in the sequence.

Process Model

A process model might posit that change in opinion is a combined function
of: (a) the individual's *initial position,* (b) his *attention* to the communicator and the message, (c) *comprehension* of its arguments, examples,
appeals and conclusion, (d) general and specific *motivation* for accepting its
position.

Attention. Obviously, before a message can be understood and reacted to, it
has to be received. Studies of the process of attention would distinguish
between factors necessary for attention-getting and those critical for atten-
tion-holding. The uniqueness of the communicator—his voice, appearance,
style, and the way he is introduced—should increase attention-getting. Similarly, the opening rhetoric of the message will increase attention to it. Its
novelty, the medium through which it is presented, its salience against a
background of competing stimuli will all affect attention-getting. On the
other hand, to hold attention, the communication must be at a level of
complexity appropriate to the audience, not so simple as to bore them or
so complex as to be incomprehensible. Beyond some point, the more effort
required to attend to the message, the less it will be attended to. External
situational distractions and some internal sources of distraction (anxiety,
daydreaming, etc.) also compete with focused attention.

Comprehension. Comprehension of the message will be influenced by aspects of its organization and structure, clarity and vividness of presentation, built-in summaries, restatement, rehearsal opportunities, and the use of the audience's language. The recipient's intelligence, relevant experience, openmindedness, "cognitive tuning set" (readiness to pass the information on, to be entertained, to be tested, etc.), all will determine whether he comprehends what he hears or reads. Comprehension can also be severely limited by intense affect related to a given attitude (to be demonstrated in Chapter 6 with an example of an extremely prejudiced woman).

Acceptance motivation. The process of acceptance is certainly at the core of the attitude-change sequence and involves many factors of costs to and utility for the recipient. Depending on the motivational basis for the individual's original attitude, his acceptance might be affected by new information which refutes his existing beliefs, by a reward for agreeing with the position, by insights into the irrational aspects of his original attitude, by fear of rejection or of being a deviant. Situational characteristics which create a positive "atmosphere" should generate a generalized response of acceptance.

Detracting from the probability that a communication will be accepted are cues which focus attention on the source's manipulative intent. Let us consider this psychological process in more detail.

Awareness of someone's intention to manipulate your behavior is often sufficient to render the influence attempt ineffectual—even when its goal is to your benefit (as a mother's goal of making her child healthy by trying to persuade him to eat nutritious foods like liver and spinach). The recipient will probably resist influence when he is *sensitized* to the assault on his attitudes: through the obviousness of a "hard sell," through pre-measures of his original attitude, or through other cues in the communicator's behavior, the message, or the setting. Instead of accepting the communication, he will muster defenses against attending to all of the message, or will refuse to do the mental work necessary to comprehend all of it, or will expend much effort silently rehearsing counterarguments during the speech, or seeking support for his original position after it. Suspicion, or paranoid-like tendencies of the recipient, may also increase the likelihood that he will perceive manipulative intent and resist it.

The refutation of the persuasive arguments through counterarguments is postulated as a central resistance mechanism, which should vary in effectiveness with one's knowledge of one's own position, clarity of the opposition, opportunity to think, expectation of a rejoinder, past experience in counter-arguing, and the time between exposure to the speech and requested overt reaction to it.

Both this process model and the "who, what, whom" model of attitude change are presented as convenient heuristic devices for the student. With their help he will be in a better position to assess, control, or systematically manipulate the variables in any program to change attitudes and behavior.

SOME GENERAL CHANGE TECHNIQUES

Before reviewing, in outline form, some of the findings which relate these variables to changes in attitudes, it might be well to mention that all techniques of attitude change rely upon the assumption that change comes out of conflict, discrepancy, inconsistency, or discontent with the status quo. Group pressure techniques make the individual aware that his behavior is in disagreement with the norms of the group. Formal communication studies create a discrepancy between where the individual is and where he ought to be to gain reinforcement, avoid punishment, or be rational. The "forced compliance" technique of using subtle pressures to induce a person to publicly engage in a behavior which is discrepant with his attitude produces self-generated changes in attitudes (see Chapter 5).

Other general techniques for changing attitudes are post-hypnotic suggestions, therapeutic interaction between a therapist and patient, social imitation of a model's behavior, and conditioning procedures. Also, it appears that mere repeated exposure to a stimulus (without reinforcement) can increase positive attitudes toward it.

SUMMARY OF SOCIAL PSYCHOLOGICAL FINDINGS[1]

A. THE PERSUADER

1. There will be more opinion change in the desired direction if the communicator has high credibility than if he has low credibility. Credibility is:

   a. Expertise (ability to know correct stand on issue).

   b. Trustworthiness (motivation to communicate knowledge without bias).

2. The credibility of the persuader is less of a factor in opinion change later on than it is immediately after exposure.

3. A communicator's effectiveness is increased if he initially expresses some views that are also held by his audience.

---

[1] Our organization and presentation of the material in this section is taken largely from Abelson (1959), now in the process of being revised by Abelson and Karlins. Support for these propositions, as well as additional findings, can be found in the following: C. I. Hovland, I. L. Janis, and H. H. Kelley, *Communication and Persuasion,* New Haven: Yale University Press, 1953; W. J. McGuire, "The Nature of Attitudes and Attitude Change," in G. L. Lindsey and E. Aronson (eds.), *The Handbook of Social Psychology,* Vol. III, Reading, Mass.: Addison-Wesley, 1969.

4. What an audience thinks of a persuader may be directly influenced by what they think of his message.

5. The more extreme the opinion change that the communicator asks for, the more actual change he is likely to get.

    a. The greater the discrepancy (between communication and recipient's initial position), the greater the attitude change, up to extremely discrepant points.

    b. With extreme discrepancy, and with low-credibility sources, there is a falling off in attitude change.

6. Communicator characteristics irrelevant to the topic of his message can influence acceptance of its conclusion.

B. HOW TO PRESENT THE ISSUES

1. Present one side of the argument when the audience is generally friendly, or when your position is the only one that will be presented, or when you want immediate, though temporary, opinion change.

2. Present both sides of the argument when the audience starts out disagreeing with you, or when it is probable that the audience will hear the other side from someone else.

3. When opposite views are presented one after another, the one presented last will probably be more effective. Primacy effect is more predominant when the second side immediately follows the first, while recency effect is more predominant when the opinion measure comes immediately after the second side.

4. There will probably be more opinion change in the direction you want if you explicitly state your conclusions than if you let the audience draw their own, except when they are rather intelligent. Then implicit conclusion drawing is better.

5. Sometimes emotional appeals are more influential, sometimes factual ones. It all depends on the kind of audience.

6. Fear appeals: The findings generally show a positive relationship between intensity of fear arousal and amount of attitude change, if recommendations for action are explicit and possible, but a negative reaction otherwise.

7. The fewer the extrinsic justifications provided in the communication for engaging in counter-norm behavior, the greater the attitude change after actual compliance.

8. No final conclusion can be drawn about whether the opening or closing parts of the communication should contain the more important material.

9. Cues which forewarn the audience of the manipulative intent of the communication increase resistance to it, while the presence of distractors simultaneously presented with the message decreases resistance.

C. THE AUDIENCE AS INDIVIDUALS

1. The people you may want most in your audience are often least likely to be there. There is evidence for selective seeking and exposure to information consonant with one's position, but not for selective avoidance of information dissonant with one's position.

2. The level of intelligence of an audience determines the effectiveness of some kinds of appeals.

3. Successful persuasion takes into account the reasons underlying attitudes as well as the attitudes themselves. That is, the techniques used must be tailored to the basis for developing the attitude.

4. The individual's personality traits affect his susceptibility to persuasion; he is more easily influenced when his self-esteem is low.

5. There are individuals who are highly persuasible and who will be easily changed by any influence attempt, but who are then equally influenceable when faced with countercommunications.

6. Ego-involvement with the content of the communication (its relation to ideological values of the audience) decreases the acceptance of its conclusion. Involvement with the consequences of one's response increases the probability of change and does so more when source-audience discrepancy is greater.

7. Actively role-playing a previously unacceptable position increases its acceptability.

D. THE INFLUENCE OF GROUPS

1. A person's opinions and attitudes are strongly influenced by groups to which he belongs and wants to belong.

2. A person is rewarded for conforming to the standards of the group and punished for deviating from them.

3. People who are most attached to the group are probably least influenced by communications which conflict with group norms.

4. Opinions which people make known to others are harder to change than opinions which people hold privately.

5. Audience participation (group discussion and decision-making) helps to overcome resistance.

6. Resistance to a counter-norm communication increases with salience of one's group identification.

7. The support of even one other person weakens the powerful effect of a majority opinion of an individual.

8. A minority of two people can influence the majority if they are consistent in their deviant responses.

E. THE PERSISTENCE OF OPINION CHANGE

1. In time, the effects of a persuasive communication tend to wear off.
   a. A communication from a positive source leads to more rapid decay of attitude change over time than one from a negative source.
   b. A complex or subtle message produces slower decay of attitude change.
   c. Attitude change is more persistent over time if the receiver actively participates in, rather than passively receives, the communication.

2. Repeating a communication tends to prolong its influence.

3. More of the desired opinion change may be found some time after exposure to the communication than right after exposure (sleeper effect).

Now we are in a somewhat better position to begin formulating specific strategies and tactics for changing attitudes. But the reader will notice that although the review of reliable findings was not intended to be exhaustive, it was skimpy compared to the number of suggested variables and complex processes involved. Two questions must be asked by the reader at this point.

First, where did these results come from, and how were they established? Second, suppose you wanted to test a hunch about how one or more of the variables we mentioned affect attitude change. What procedures could you employ to produce findings in which you could place your confidence? Unless you can do so, you will be unable to incorporate them into your attitude change technology. The next chapter offers the answers to these questions.

CHAPTER THREE

Examining the Experiment as a General Source of Information, and Reviewing Some Representative Studies

Although we saw in the previous chapter that there are many types of research which provide information relevant to the modification of attitudes, our primary focus in this book centers upon the use of the formal experiment in communication and attitude change.[1] Before examining a sample of such studies, let us outline some of the distinguishing characteristics of this type of research.

Individual subjects are exposed to a communication administered under controlled conditions where one or more features of the situation are systematically varied. The persuasive effects of the communication and the effectiveness of the manipulated independent variable(s) are then evaluated in terms of the direction and magnitude of observed attitude change.

The communication. A message is constructed by the experimenter which advocates a position discrepant from that of the intended audience, and which contains supporting arguments, evidence, and implications. Usually there is only a single, relatively short message of unitary direction and organization.

---

[1] For students unfamiliar with the distinguishing characteristics of an experiment, we have included in Postscript B a compact analysis of what an experiment is and why it is such a valuable source of information about physical and social reality.

The issues or topic communicated. With few exceptions, the communication deals with issues which are not ego-involving for the subjects. The attitudes are rarely socially significant ones, nor are they based upon extensive prior experience or personal commitment. Hovland (1959) cogently describes the rationale for this feature of the attitude-change experiment: "We usually deliberately try to find types of issues involving attitudes which are susceptible to modification through communication. Otherwise, we run the risk of no measurable effects, particularly with small-scale experiments." (p. 10)

The source. Typically the source of the communication is explicitly stated, as when the message is attributed to a specific person or known organization. In cases where it is not explicit, there is usually implicit endorsement of the message by the researcher or person in charge of the group (e.g., a teacher, or an official in the organization to which the subjects belong). This legitimization of the message by the researcher's sponsorship increases the likelihood that subjects will view the advocated position as one that is reasonable, or at least worthy of consideration.

The setting. An experiment is a novel situation for the subjects, because they are often in an unfamiliar place (such as a laboratory) and are engaging in unfamiliar behavior. Thus the usual social supports for their original attitude position are not available, since it is not possible for them to talk to other subjects, to question the experimenter, or to obtain more information than is given in the communication. The setting is designed to guarantee the saliency of the communication above all other possible stimuli. There are no competing messages, background distractions are minimized, and a serious, test-like atmosphere is created.

The audience. Subjects are most often college students who participate in order to obtain money or course credit, or who volunteer just out of intellectual curiosity. Once they are in the experimental room, they are a "captive" audience, with only "extrinsic" justification for being there. They have not come to hear a speech, but rather to obtain rewards which are totally irrelevant to the communication itself. They are generally more intelligent, more highly motivated, and better able to critically analyze the logical structure of a communication than individuals from a non-college population.

Exposure to the communication. With the use of captive audiences there is no problem of subject self-selection. That is, the audience is *not* composed of only those who want to hear this particular speech; rather, it is made up of people with a variety of attitudes toward the communication. However, there is no assurance that the audience in an experiment will attend to the communication, or that there will not be self-selection in exposure to some or most of its content.

Behavior measurement. Three general response measures are included in most of these experiments: (1) a check on the efficacy of the independent variable, (2) a measure of comprehension or retention of the message, and (3) a measure of attitude toward the position advocated.

For the first of these measurements, the experimenter collects information on whether or not the subject appropriately perceived the stimulus conditions defined as the independent variable. For example, was the subject made anxious by an anxiety-arousal manipulation, or were differences in communicator credibility between two sources perceived veridically by the subject?

Sometimes there is a lack of agreement between the way in which the experimenters and the subjects label the independent variable. In this case, the effect of the independent variable on attitude change is examined in terms of the subject's definition of the stimulus conditions and not according to the experimenter's random assignment of subjects to different treatments. This is called an *internal analysis* because subjects *within* each treatment group who respond differently to the independent variable are compared in their reaction on the dependent measure. Such a procedure only establishes correlations between two sets of responses and not the sort of causal relation uncovered by differences between treatment groups. However, internal analyses can provide additional support for one's hypothesis, salvage an hypothesis when there are weak between-group treatments, or suggest possible sources of complexity between variables or in the manipulations. It should be noted that conclusions based on an internal analysis must be subsequently replicated in further experiments employing only between-group analyses.

Comprehension and retention of the message are usually measured quite simply by multiple-choice, objective response tests administered after the message is completed.

Attitudes toward the advocated position are determined by self-report opinion scales in which the subject describes the degree to which he endorses a particular verbal statement. His agreement with the position is usually represented by placing his response at some point along an affective dimension (often from "Like X extremely," through a point of neutrality, to "Dislike X extremely"). Opinions may be measured both before and after the communication, in order to obtain a measure of individual change. If they are only measured after the communication, they are compared with the after-only scores of a no-communication control group in order to determine the effect of the communication. However, we might note here that when there is a pre-measure of attitude, the experimenter often tries to conceal the relationship between it and the experimental influence attempt. He may do this by separating them in time, or by using different physical locations, research personnel, and rationales for data collection.

Time. In laboratory studies of attitude change, the time spent in the entire experiment is not very long (usually about one hour). The duration of the communication is brief, and the time between exposure to it and measures of retention or opinion change is a matter of minutes. Thus, most conclusions have to be limited to immediate or short-term effects, unless the time dimension is manipulated.

Now that you have some idea about what is special about research on attitude change, you are in a better position to review and evaluate a representative sample of studies in this area. The studies to be presented reflect different research approaches, utilized to test ideas which come from a variety of sources.

THE INFLUENCE OF SOURCE CREDIBILITY
ON COMMUNICATION EFFECTIVENESS

The question of how to produce a large amount of change in the attitudes of an audience has been studied quite extensively. To rephrase the problem, let us suppose that we have decided to use a formal communication (a speech or persuasive verbal message) as our main method of producing attitude change. How can we, without changing the structure or content of the communication, increase the amount of this change? It may actually be that the only thing which affects the amount of attitude change is the communication itself. But if not, what extra-communication variables are likely to increase such change, and why? One variable which we intuitively feel should affect attitude change is the source of the communication.

It seems likely that a trustworthy source, giving the same persuasive message as an untrustworthy source, would produce more attitude change. Although it does appear intuitively obvious, we can still ask how much *more* change a trustworthy source produces than an untrustworthy source. Another interesting question is whether or not untrustworthy sources produce attitude change in the opposite direction from the communication. To adequately and accurately answer these and any other questions on the effect of source credibility, it is necessary to conduct an experiment. Hovland and Weiss (1951) conducted a study which was intended to answer just such questions.

The design of the study was quite simple. The subjects, undergraduate college students at Yale University who were in an advanced history course, filled out an opinion questionnaire a week before receiving persuasive communications. For some subjects, the communicators associated with particular communications were trustworthy, while for others they were untrustworthy. Immediately after the communications were presented, another opinion questionnaire was administered. Finally, a third opinion questionnaire was filled out one month later.

Keeping the overall design in mind, the details of the study were as follows. Five days after the administration of the first opinion questionnaire (designed to be a general opinion survey conducted by the "National Opinion Survey Council"), one of the experimenters entered the history class as a guest lecturer. The fact that he was a guest lecturer, who had never come to class before, was meant to dissociate his activities from the previous opinion questionnaire. He stated that he had been asked by the regular professor to discuss the psychology of communications with the class, since so many of their attitudes and opinions were determined by what they heard and read. He then added that before he talked with the class, he wished to have "live data" from a survey which attempted to assess the role of newspaper and magazine reading as a vehicle of communication. After obtaining these data, he would discuss them with the class at a later session. The lecturer continued by summarizing what he wished the class to do: namely, read a few newspaper and magazine articles on controversial topics, which were based on the best available information. After reading the articles, the students would be expected to fill out a short questionnaire on their reactions to them.

Each student was then handed a booklet of four readings on four different controversial issues:

A.   Should the anti-histamine drugs continue to be sold without a doctor's prescription?

B.   Can a practicable atomic-powered submarine be built at the present time (1949-50)?

C.   Is the steel industry to blame for the current shortage of steel?

D.   As a result of TV, will there be a decrease in the number of movie theaters in operation by 1955?

For each topic, respectively, the high and low "credibility" sources were:

High	Low
A. *New England Journal of Biology and Medicine*	Magazine *A* (a mass circulation, monthly pictorial magazine)
B. Robert J. Oppenheimer	*Pravda*
C. *Bulletin of National Resources Planning Board*	Writer *A* (a widely syndicated, anti-labor, anti-New Deal, "rightist" newspaper columnist)
D. *Fortune*	Writer *B* (an extensively syndicated, woman movie-gossip columnist)

For each topic there were both pro and con versions of the communication. Each booklet contained two pro and two con communications, one on each topic, and one pro communication and one con communication attributed to a low-credibility source. The other two communications were attributed to high-credibility sources. All the communications on a topic were identical, differing only in the attributed source. There was a total of

TABLE 3.1

Percent of Subjects Rating Source as Trustworthy
(Adapted from Hovland and Weiss, 1951)

Topic	High credibility	Low credibility
A	95	6
B	94	1
C	81	17
D	89	21

twenty-four different booklets, with different combinations of topic, source, and advocated position.

After the subjects had read the booklets, they were given a second questionnaire which differed in format from the previous opinion survey. This questionnaire first asked general questions about the subjects' reactions to the articles and then asked for their own opinions. At the end of the questionnaire, there was a multiple-choice, fact quiz. The final questionnaire, given one month later, was identical to the second one (in order to assess delayed effects). However, the very first questionnaire, in addition to asking opinion questions, asked the subjects to rate many sources for trustworthiness. Included among these sources were the ones actually used in the experiment.

In considering the results of the experiment, we would first want to know how trustworthy the subjects judged the various sources. Did they indeed see the high-credibility sources as more trustworthy than the low-credibility sources? To answer this question, the ratings from the very first opinion survey can be used. The results can be seen in Table 3.1. A cursory glance at these results overwhelmingly confirms the hope that the high-credibility sources were seen as more trustworthy than the low-credibility sources.

What about attitude change? In order to consider the amount of attitude change produced, we have to be able to summarize the data. The summary technique used in this experiment was to take the percent of subjects who changed their attitude (from questionnaire 1 to questionnaire 2) in the direction of the communication and subtract from that the percent of subjects who changed in the opposite direction from the communication. Thus, if the communication were pro, the percent changing in the pro direction minus the percent changing in the con direction would be our measure (net change) of the amount of attitude change produced. The net changes of opinion in the direction of the communication for sources judged to be trustworthy or untrustworthy are presented in Table 3.2.

These results show that the *difference* between the average (across topics) net change for the trustworthy sources and the untrustworthy sources was 14.1 percent. The probability of this difference being caused by

TABLE 3.2

Net Changes of Opinion in Direction of Communication for Sources Judged Trustworthy or Untrustworthy by Individual Subjects
(Adapted from Hovland and Weiss, 1951)

Topic	Net change (percentage)	
	Sources judged trustworthy	Sources judged untrustworthy
A	25.5	11.1
B	36.0	0.6
C	18.2	7.4
D	12.9	17.2
Average change	22.5%	8.4%

chance is .03 (i.e., it would occur by chance only 3 times in 100); thus this difference appears to be a real one. That is, subjects are more likely to change their attitudes in the direction of a communication if they think that it came from a trustworthy source, than if they think it came from an untrustworthy one.

But why does a trustworthy source produce more change? Do the subjects pay more attention to him and thus learn the arguments better? Data from the fact quiz in the second questionnaire indicated that there was no difference between the trustworthy and untrustworthy source conditions in the amount of information recalled about the communications.

In conclusion, it seems that intuition proved to be correct. An experiment demonstrated that more attitude change was produced by a persuasive message if the message were attributed to high-credibility sources than if it were attributed to low-credibility sources. The magnitude of the difference in attitude change produced by the different communicators was fairly large. In addition, the low-credibility sources seemed to produce a low net percent of attitude change (8.4%). To summarize, more attitude change follows from a formal communication if the source is trustworthy than if the source is untrustworthy. Further, untrustworthy sources seem to produce little, if any, attitude change.

THE INFLUENCE OF ROLE-PLAYING ON OPINION CHANGE

The previously discussed hypothesis was derived from an intuitive consideration of the events that ought to produce more or less attitude change. However, there are other sources, besides intuition, which can be used to derive such hypotheses. One method is to consider variables that have been studied in other areas of psychology. For example, the technique of role-playing has been used for producing changes in a person's personality. By role-playing behavior which normally he would not have performed, the person is assumed to gain insight into how others see him and how he might behave. In other words, the person gets to see the world from another point of view by acting as if he had a different attitude. If it can be assumed that the role-playing of an attitude position contrary to one's own supplies new insight into that position, it might be possible to use this technique to produce attitude change. Janis and King (1954) conducted an experiment to determine whether role-playing was a more or less effective attitude change technique than just passive listening.

Role-playing, like source credibility, is an extra-communication variable. That is, in testing the difference between role-playing and passive listening, the experimenter would want to make sure that the same communication content and structure were used for each method. In the credibility study this was accomplished by attaching different source names to the same communication. However, for role-playing variables, the experimenter cannot merely ask some subjects to role-play and others to listen to a communication. This is because subjects who are role-playing may use persuasive arguments that are different from what the listening subjects receive. If this happened, the experimenters would not know whether a difference in attitude change was due to the role-playing itself, or to the different arguments used.

To control for this possibility, Janis and King used three communication topics, and tested subjects three at a time. Each subject had to role-play an attitude position on one topic and listen to the remaining two subjects role-play the attitude position on the other topics. Thus, each subject passively listened to two communications. However, these latter communications were constructed from the role-playing speeches of the two other subjects. This point might be clarified by describing their procedure in more detail.

The overall design of this study was similar to that used by Hovland and Weiss. Four weeks before the experimental sessions, an opinion questionnaire was administered to a college class. Embedded in the questionnaire were three key opinion items: the number of movie theaters that would be in existence three years hence, the total meat supply available to the United States in 1953, and the number of years it would take to find a cure for the common cold. The subjects' rating of the number of theaters, amount of meat, and number of years constitutes the opinion measure.

When the three subjects arrived at the experimental session, they were led to believe that they were taking part in a research project which had been designed to develop aptitude tests for assessing oral speaking ability. They were then given an outline which contained information relating to one of the three topics. The outline included arguments advocating lower numerical opinion estimates than those previously given by the subjects (thus constituting the discrepant position). With these outlines as a guide, the subjects were asked to give informal talks. While one of the three subjects gave his talk, the other two listened. Thus each subject gave one talk and heard two. After the third talk was completed, the subjects were asked to fill out a second questionnaire which contained self-rating items about performances, and about their opinions on the topics.

The results of this experiment can be stated rather simply. For two topics (movie theaters and meat supply) the role-playing subjects changed their opinions more in the direction of the communication than did the passive listening subjects. For the common cold topic there was no difference in the amount of attitude change produced by the two methods. Furthermore, all of the changes in attitude were in the direction of the communications.

These results present a problem for us. If we wanted to use this role-playing technique to produce attitude change, we could never be sure that it would be the most effective method since, in this experiment, the role-playing technique worked for only two of the three topics. How can we determine why role-playing was less effective for the topic of curing colds? Fortunately, Janis and King used a good general technique at the end of each experimental session which supplied them with some hypotheses about this problem. The technique they used was an extended interview with each subject. After the subjects had completed the second questionnaire, they were interviewed about their reactions to the entire experiment. From the interview, the researchers found out that the subjects who had to talk on the cold cure issue tended to be less *satisfied* with their role-playing performance than subjects who gave talks on the other issues. Thus the effectiveness of role-playing may depend on how satisfied the subjects feel about their performance. However, we cannot be sure that this is true. It is only an interesting hypothesis based on informally gathered data. To check on its validity, a second experiment was conducted by King and Janis (1956).

The purpose of this second study was to see if the crucial factor in producing attitude change by role-playing was the satisfaction felt by subjects when they improvised well. To test whether such satisfaction was more effective than improvisation by itself, King and Janis conducted a three-group experiment. Only one topic was used (students were asked to believe that at least 90 percent of college students would be drafted after graduation, and once drafted they would have to serve three year's military duty). In one group, subjects used an outline to improvise a speech (which was tape-recorded by the experimenter). In another group, subjects merely read a similar prepared speech into a tape-recorder. In the third group, subjects silently read the prepared speech to themselves.

From the results of this experiment, the authors concluded that more attitude change was produced in the direction of the communication when the subjects improvised, than when they either read aloud or to themselves.

Furthermore, since subjects in the reading aloud condition were more satisfied with their performance than subjects in the improvisation condition, King and Janis concluded that improvisation was more important than satisfaction for producing attitude change.

In conclusion, these two studies seem to suggest that the role-playing of attitude positions counter to one's own can be a powerful technique in producing attitude change.

FIELD STUDIES OF PERSONAL INFLUENCE

Our understanding of the attitude change process can also benefit from a very different method for getting ideas. Katz and Lazarsfeld (1955) used an interview survey technique to uncover the sources in a person's life which have the greatest influence on his decisions. They did not start with hypotheses to be tested or independent variables to be manipulated. Rather, they began with a series of questions which they posed to 800 families in the midwest city of Decatur, Illinois (population of 60,000 at the time of the study). From their responses, many hypotheses can be devised about techniques for changing attitudes and behavior.

In a large-scale influence attempt (as might be used in a birth control program), where should the emphasis be placed—on direct persuasion of individuals or on indirect persuasion of them through the use of familiar sources? These researchers provide data which show that a person's immediate family is responsible for two-thirds of all the specific influence attempts on him, and for one-half of the more general kinds of influence.

Starting with information such as this, we could make better decisions about the directed locus of our change attempt. Clearly, to effect a specific change in any given person, the communicator should do so indirectly by first reaching the members of the person's family. To produce a more general change in his behavior, there would be no advantage in working through his family rather than through mass media.

What is the best medium to employ for getting our message to the person, and guaranteeing that it will be attended to? Results from these studies suggest that magazine advertisements are least effective, while the most effective medium is interpersonal communication between people known to each other.

If people are most likely to allow themselves to be *exposed* to communications delivered directly by other people, are there certain others who are most influential in getting them to *accept* the message? Katz and Lazarsfeld found that in each community there were *opinion leaders* who exerted a strong effect upon the formation and change of opinions in other people. These opinion leaders were the significant mediators in any persuasion attempt, standing between the primary source of influence and the eventual target audience.

This "two-step flow of communication" was nicely illustrated in a study of how doctors are persuaded to prescribe a new drug for their patients. Most of the doctors were unwilling to be innovators or accept the advice from drug salesmen directly. Rather, they waited to be persuaded by opinion leaders among their medical colleagues. Other doctors, who were willing to take more risk in being first to prescribe the drug, exerted a very powerful effect upon the majority of doctors who could not be influenced by the salesmen's "pitch." Incidentally, in this study, a very interesting "nonobvious" measure of change was used: the actual druggist's records of which doctors prescribed the drug at which time after it was introduced.

Opinion leaders like these exist for various subgroups within a community, and this study indicates that they should be the initial targets of persuasion. It is also noteworthy that they are not necessarily the "sociometric stars," the ones most liked by the majority of others in their group. In order to single them out, or to create new opinion leaders, more research is necessary to establish the essential ingredients which make up an effective opinion leader.

This type of field research gives us many hunches worth following up, but they are only informed speculations which must be subjected to the controlled testing procedures of the experiment. Appropriate experimental designs can help isolate the specific components of a general concept which are the effective causal agents in the process. The next example shows how this can be done.

TRACKING DOWN THE EFFECTS OF DISTRACTION

One aspect of the scientific approach is its continual search for the way things really are. Because of this, scientists view specific problems in two ways. They are both critical and creative at the same time. First, they develop ideas about how something *ought* to work. We have seen that these ideas come from intuition, from other areas of psychology, from general systematic observation of a problem area, and (as seen in Chapter 5) from theories. More often than not, these ideas lead to an experiment which is designed to test a specific hypothesis (e.g., the role of credibility in attitude change).

But after finishing an experiment, where do scientists find their next hypothesis? Typically, they *critically evaluate* their own work and the related research of other scientists. They ask themselves whether these experiments have conclusively demonstrated that a particular finding is true. If there is any doubt, new hypotheses are created to explain the questionable results. A good example of this chain of events in social psychology is the research which has been done on the effect of *distraction* on attitude change.

In 1961, Allyn and Festinger conducted an experiment which was originally designed to test the following hypothesis: when subjects are forewarned that a communication has been especially designed to change their attitudes, the effect of that communication is reduced. An obvious test of this hypothesis would be to forewarn one group of subjects and not another, and to then present both groups with the same communication designed to change the subjects' attitudes. Allyn and Festinger did just this. A speech was given to high-school students which suggested that the driving age in California be raised from 16 to 21. Half of the students were asked to pay attention to the message, which was going to be about the menace of teenage driving (forewarning). The other half of the students were asked to pay attention to the speaker's personality but were not told the topic of the speech (no forewarning). Two main measures were taken: a pre-post opinion change score (similar to that used by Hovland and Weiss), and a measure of the number of students who thought that the speaker was biased in his presentation.

The results from these measures were in line with the hypothesis. That is, subjects who were not forewarned changed their opinion more towards the direction of the communication than subjects who were forewarned. Furthermore, subjects who were forewarned said more often that the communicator was biased than subjects who were not forewarned (80 percent vs. 61 percent). This experiment appeared to be good support for the notion that if one wishes to produce large changes in attitude, it would be best *not* to forewarn people of one's intention to do so.

Festinger and Maccoby (1964) critically examined this study and asked whether or not the experiment did indeed unambiguously support the forewarning conclusion. They found that there was another difference between the two groups of subjects in addition to the forewarning which may have caused the attitude change. One group of subjects was told to attend to the speaker's personality (and was not forewarned), while the other group was told to attend to the message (and was forewarned). The former subjects may have been so distracted by attending to the speaker's personality that they could not think of counterarguments against what the speaker was saying. As a result, these distracted subjects may have accepted the communication more easily than the forewarned subjects. By criticizing the first study, Festinger and Maccoby derived a new hypothesis: If people are *distracted* while listening to a communication, they will change their attitudes more in the direction of the communication than if they are not distracted.

To test this hypothesis, two groups of students listened to a communication which argued against college fraternities. Along with the communication one group saw a film of the speaker giving the talk, while the other group saw a rather amusing silent comedy film (distraction condition). In general, the results supported the hypothesis. The distraction condition produced more attitude change in the direction of the communication (against fraternities) than the no-distraction condition.

What about forewarning without distraction? A study by Freedman and Sears (1965) proceeded to demonstrate that both distraction alone and forewarning alone were important variables in attitude change. They asked subjects to either attend to the content of a speech (no distraction) or to the personality of the speaker (distraction). Half of each of these groups of subjects were forewarned about the nature of the communication, while the other half were not forewarned. The authors found that distraction increased the amount of attitude change, while forewarning decreased it.

But what psychological processes operate to make distraction effective in augmenting attitude change? A number of recent studies have tried to answer this question by analyzing how the distraction manipulation might have worked in the previous studies.

If opportunity to counterargue while listening to a persuasive speech decreases its acceptance, then perhaps distraction is effective because it limits counterarguing. Indeed, McGuire and Papageorgis (1962) found that sensitizing their audience to counterarguments before hearing a persuasive communication resulted in lessened attitude change.

In the studies described earlier, the distraction manipulation focused the audience's attention on the speaker's personality. If he was a credible communicator, then this operational definition of distraction may have simply made more salient his credibility and only indirectly affected distraction. One cannot be sure of such an explanation because credibility was not varied; rather it was constant across conditions. From the instructions and setting used in these studies, it is likely, however, that the communicator was perceived as credible.

When the same distraction manipulation was again used (by Miller and Baron, 1968) but, in addition, the communicator's credibility was explicitly varied, distraction had two different effects upon attitude change. Where it was coupled with a credible communicator (i.e., it presumably called attention to him) most change occurred. On the other hand, when it was combined with the noncredible communicator treatment, least attitude change resulted.

If it were possible to manipulate distraction without possible contamination with other independent variables, then it should be the case that the more distracting the stimulus conditions, the greater the change produced. If a little distraction produces a small change, then a powerful distractor ought to yield sizable change in attitudes.

In reflecting upon this possibility, it is well to also think about the nature of distractions as they occur in real life. If you were listening to an important message, there would rarely be *external* distractors present which could not be easily eliminated. However, what about *internal* distractors, such as states of anxiety, disgust, love and passion? These are not so easily brushed aside while you are supposed to be attending to the presentation of important information. To the point is a recent study by Cameron, Frank, Lifter, and Morrissey (1968) of student attention during a lecture. It revealed that 60 percent of the time the students were not listening—even though the lecturer was very good. Moreover, they reported that about a fourth of the time they were engaged in daydreaming sexual fantasies.

Suppose subjects were implicitly encouraged to generate sexual fantasies while they were being exposed to a persuasive communication about a topic totally unrelated to this mental-emotional activity. Would the message have more of a chance of getting in, and persuading them, than if they were not distracted by such intense, presumably positive affect?

To explore this possibility, an experiment was performed (Zimbardo, Ebbesen, and Fraser, 1968) which attempted to arouse strong sexual motivation among male college subjects while they listened to a formal communication. The ostensible purpose of the study was to test "bi-modal sensory input processing," a psycho-physiological process in which different sense modes are stimulated simultaneously. This "front" allowed the researchers to justify the concurrent auditory (message) and visual (distraction) stimulation given each subject.

A three-minute tape-recorded speech which advocated a position discrepant from that of the subjects' (previously measured) was played while they watched innocuous slides of scenery. Accompanying a second persuasive speech (similar in structure but on a different topic than the first) were slides of female nudes in rather sexually provocative poses.

The results were quite clear; the presence of a sexual distractor made the message more potent. It produced more change in attitude than did a message presented with an affectively neutral distractor. This was true even though the subjects were able to recall less of the content of the communication accompanied by provocative slides than of the communication accompanied by scenery.

While this study tends to support the positive relationship previously found between distraction and attitude change, it also raises the obvious next question: do affectively *negative* distractors have the same effect? Essentially the same research design and methodology were used in a second study by these investigators. This time, however, female subjects were shown a series of colorful medical slides of postmortems, dismembered limbs, patients dying from third-degree burns, etc. It was assumed that such stimuli would arouse a variety of strong emotions which could be characterized as negative affect. One other difference between the two studies is that in this one there were three treatments. Each subject first received a persuasive communication without a distractor (actually she read the communication while also listening to it). Then half the co-eds got the gory slides along with a second communication, while half received the affectively neutral distractor (scenery slides) with the communication.

Although it was shown that the medical slides did create a powerful internal source of distraction, this condition resulted in least attitude change. Relative to the no-distraction baseline for change, this group changed significantly less than did those with the neutral distractor. Thus it is not distraction *per se* which makes a communication more effective, nor its intensity; rather it is in part a function of the affective reaction produced in the audience by the distractor.

We have not presented all of the research which has been directed toward evaluating and clarifying the status of distraction as an independent variable and as a process in the attitude change sequence. However, even from this small set of studies, one can see the cumulative development of ideas in the scientific approach to finding out the nature of psychological reality. Psychologists are continually evaluating their experiments so that they can create new hypotheses about both established and novel phenomena. Furthermore, such a critical evaluation leads to the refinement of vaguely conceived previous notions, as well as to the generation of new ones. Thus, the history of a science is the fertile ground from which grow the hypotheses and laws of the future. One of the best techniques to insure speedy and accurate growth in a science is to be critical. In the next chapter we will examine this technique more closely, so that we may be better able to evaluate previous research and single out those ideas which have important implications for an effective practical program of attitude change.

CHAPTER FOUR

Critically Analyzing the Conceptualization, Methodology, and Interpretation of Attitude Change Research

When an engineer applies principles derived from research in physics to the practical problem of designing and building a bridge, he allows for a margin of error in his extrapolation from the experimental evidence. This "safety factor" is necessary because the laboratory test conditions can only approximate the unique features of the actual field situation. The magnitude of the safety factor would be greater as the evidence from research becomes less convincing, as the expected utilization of the bridge is greater, and as there is more money and time available to expend in construction. Even with repeatedly substantiated empirical evidence as an operating base, the engineer still employs a large safety factor.

The approach we have developed in this book casts the reader in the role of a behavioral engineer intent upon building a useful technology of attitude change. How will you estimate the safety factor necessary to minimize the risks involved in extending the experimental evidence from attitude change studies to the real life situation you are attempting to influence?

There are at least two steps to such an estimation process. First, you will have to determine the soundness of the evidence provided for you by the research in a relevant field. This must be done in order to evaluate how much confidence you are willing to invest in the conclusions of such research. Secondly, once you have established some reasonable level of confidence, you must estimate the extent to which the findings suffer (are stretched) to fit the particular application you have in mind.

This chapter will begin to provide you with the critical orientation which you will need to accomplish the first of these goals. Of necessity, we cannot deal directly with the second issue unless we know a great deal about the specific features of the practical problem of concern.

However, in the final chapter, when we analyze several concrete instances of applied attitude change procedures, there will be a glimpse of the problems confronted, and the compromises necessary, in trying to systematically change the attitudes and behavior of people in the world outside the laboratory.

Four studies will be placed under analytical scrutiny: two which have just been described to you (nonevaluatively) in the previous chapter, and two new ones. We believe that many important aspects of design, execution, analysis, and interpretation may be demonstrated from an intensive examination of these particular studies. Our purpose in this next section is not to diminish the creative contribution of the researchers whose studies are presented. Rather we will suggest that a serious student must adopt a general orientation of *critical acceptance* if he expects to have a firm basis on which to start developing his own technology.

THE GRASSHOPPER EXPERIMENT

Let us apply such a critical orientation to a particularly imaginative experiment (Smith, 1961a). In so doing, we should note what happens to our understanding of the attitude change process when the experiment has problems in its design, procedure, and analysis.

An attempt was made to change the attitudes of Army reservists toward eating fried Japanese grasshoppers, by utilizing several different influence techniques. In one condition, a respected leader presented a persuasive communication; in a second, humor was introduced into the situation while a group was exposed to the food; in a third, a positive communicator induced the men to eat a grasshopper; in a fourth, the communicator was negative; while in the fifth, there was no influence attempt. We should be able to compare the relative efficacy of these different approaches for changing strongly held attitudes (of aversion) in a noncollege population studied in its natural environment (on a reservist base at a regular weekly meeting).

We will begin by describing the procedure in the author's words.[1] Then, on the basis of our analysis, we will try to predict what results are reasonable to expect. Finally, we will compare our expectations with the obtained results.

---

[1] Smith, E. E. Methods for changing consumer attitudes: A report of three experiments. Project Report, Quartermaster Food and Container Institute for the Armed Forces (PRA Report 61-2). February 1961. Reprinted by permission of The Matrix Corporation.

All groups were brought into the reserve center's kitchen area by a sergeant and seated around a large table. Throughout the experimental period fresh coffee was available and the men helped themselves to it. The experimenter introduced himself, gave a brief statement on what the experiment was about, and had them fill out the first page of the questionnaire. The experimental variation was then introduced, after which they were exposed to the grasshoppers. After they had finished eating, they finished the questionnaire. The experimenter then thanked them for their cooperation, asked them not to discuss the experiment with others, and excused them. The experiment lasted about forty minutes. The specific instructions and experimental variations in the five conditions were as follows:

In every group and experimental condition the experimental period started with the following statement being read by the experimenter:

"Good evening. I am Dr.____and I am doing research for the Army Quartermaster on food acceptance. The Army wants to find out more about how the men feel about new, different, or unusual foods, because the new Army will consist of smaller, more mobile units than we had in World War II. These new units will be more on their own, without all the support personnel and field kitchens that we had before. So the kinds of food you'll have to eat, if you want to survive, may not be as good as they were before. You may have to eat food that you may not have eaten before, and live off the land more. So tonight we are going to find out what your attitudes and reactions are toward an unusual food that you might have to eat in an emergency. This food is grasshoppers."

After reading this statement, the experimenter handed out the three-page questionnaire and had the subjects fill out the first page, which included a rating scale on grasshoppers as a food. After they had completed the first page of the questionnaire, the experimenter then read the following statement in every condition: "This is a voluntary experiment, and no one has to eat grasshoppers if they don't want to." At this point, the instructions and procedures varied according to the experimental condition, as follows.

(a) Respected leader. In this condition, after having made the statement that this was a voluntary experiment quoted above, the experimenter said, "I would like Sergeant____to tell you the importance of soldiers being willing to live off the land and eat strange foods."

At this point, a sergeant who had been selected on the advice of the officers as being highly respected by the men, in each case, a man with considerable years of experience as indicated by his hash marks and campaign ribbons, gave the men a talk in his own words on why they should learn to eat survival foods such as grasshoppers. In each case the experimenter had spoken to the sergeant prior to the experiment, and given him a rough outline of a survival talk that could be utilized. The sergeants took to this quite naturally, and generally used the same format, beginning with a statement as to the situation that soldiers often get into in which they are not amply supplied when pinned down by the enemy or isolated, and why it is necessary for them to eat strange and unusual foods that they would not ordinarily eat. They then gave examples of situations in previous wars in which they had eaten strange foods, stating that this had been necessary for their survival. They then concluded by stating that the men were fortunate to have this chance to learn to eat some of these survival foods. They concluded their talk by eating a grasshopper.

The experimenter suggested the survival approach to the sergeants but left it up to them to put it into their own words. This was done in order to make the leader influence condition, as a bench mark condition, as similar as possible to the manner in which influence attempts are normally made by NCO's to the men in the Armed Forces.

(b) Humor. In this condition, after having made the statement that this was a voluntary experiment quoted above, the experimenter stated, 'To make this meeting more pleasant, I am going to play a record for you while you eat.' The experimenter then put on the Bob Newhart record 'The Buttondown Mind Strikes Back,' at the particularly funny section on the 'Grace L. Ferguson Airline and Storm Door Company.' After the group had responded to the record with at least one good laugh, the experimenter presented them with an open can of grasshoppers and said, 'Now go ahead and eat.' The record continued to play until the men had finished eating.

(c) No influence control. There was no experimental manipulation in this condition, the subjects simply being told, after the statement quoted above that this was a voluntary experiment, "Now go ahead and eat."

(d) Positive communicator. In this condition, the experimenter acted in a friendly, warm, permissive manner throughout the experimental period. Operationally, this consisted of frequently smiling, referring to himself as Smitty rather than Dr. Smith, sitting on the counter rather than standing, saying that the men could smoke if they wished, that they should relax and enjoy themselves, etc.

In addition, in this condition as in the negative communicator condition, after stating that the experiment was voluntary, as quoted above, the experimenter said, "However, in order to get as many people as possible to try one, I will pay, right now, fifty cents to each person who eats one."

While saying this, the experimenter took a handful of quarters out of his pocket, showing them to the subjects, and paid fifty cents to every man who ate a grasshopper. It was explained that it was only necessary to eat one grasshopper to earn the fifty cents. After all those who wished to eat a grasshopper for fifty cents had done so and received their money, the experimenter said, "Now go ahead and eat."

(e) Negative communicator. In this condition, the experimenter acted in a formal, cool, official manner throughout the experimental period. Operationally, this consisted of ordering rather than requesting, telling the men they couldn't smoke, never smiling, standing in a stiff pose, replying in a sharp manner to questions, etc. (Taken from Smith, 1961, pp. 13-17.)

In addition, the experimenter told the men in this condition, as he had those in the positive communicator condition, about the fifty cents' incentive, and then proceeded as he had done in that condition.

DEPENDENT VARIABLES MEASURED

The four major responses measured were: the number of grasshoppers eaten; attitudes toward eating grasshoppers (on a nine-point "hedonic" rating scale ranging from "dislike extremely" to "like extremely"); satisfaction with the group (on a twelve-item, seven-point Likert scale, which "is very sensitive to ephemeral group feeling tones," p. 18); and ratings of the positive and negative communicator (on a seven-point Likert-type scale of responses to the single item, "the instructor was friendly and courteous").

DESIGN PROBLEMS

Problems of experimental design are found in many parts of this experiment. Let us proceed to examine them.

Control Group

This group may have been partly persuaded to eat grasshoppers by the original communication, which gave logical reasons for eating them. You might call this the "soft-sell." Also, the high degree of choice (whether to eat grasshoppers or not), in a normally authoritarian environment, may have made the subjects feel relatively autonomous, self-satisfied, inclined to try the strange food, and thus more receptive to the possibility of liking it.

The Respected Leader

This man was selected by *officers' ratings* rather than by the subjects themselves. Obviously, a discrepancy may have existed between the subjects' perceptions and the officers' perceptions of what a respected sergeant was!

In addition, the sergeant concluded his "own words" talk to the men by eating a grasshopper. If he was, in fact, respected by the men, the men would be likely to imitate him and eat a grasshopper. On the other hand, if, as was likely, he was not respected, his act may have been perceived as "calling their bluff," "an attempt to show them up," etc. This latter alternative, coupled with the likelihood that army reservists seldom listen to speeches by their noncoms, would lead to minimal effectiveness of this technique.

Humor Treatment

The failure to fit this manipulation into some overall rationale which would be meaningful to the subjects makes it a source of confusion to the men. As soon as they give one good laugh, a can of grasshoppers is shoved at them and they are told to eat! Contrary to the experimenter's expectation, the humor manipulation should produce the most ambiguity, least personal satisfaction (remember that this funny record is being played by a doctor during an official reserve meeting), and very little attitude change.

Definition of Positive and Negative Communicators

Possibly these communicators were perceived differently by the subjects than the experimenter had expected. When the "positive" communicator, a man with authority and expertise, acts cheerful, informal, and permissive in an army setting, the reservists are likely to react with caution, even suspicion. When the "negative" communicator acts cool, official, and stiff, this is just what soldiers expect, and they feel relatively comfortable. Thus subjective reactions to these different communicators may not have been very different as measured by a check on the manipulation. In addition, the experimenter's positive role did not follow as well from the introductory statement as did his negative role. A further difficulty would be the varying interpretations put by the subjects on the offer of fifty cents (an inducement? a bribe?).

PROCEDURAL PROBLEMS

Contagion and the Unit of Measurement

Since the subjects were tested in groups of about ten men (buddies from the same unit) who sat around a large table, they were in a free interaction situation in which social contagion effects and group pressures could play a major role in determining public *conformity* behavior. Such conditions of testing allow for the operation of extraneous sources of pressure, other than those attributable to the specific communicator and the manipulated variables. In any single testing session these uncontrolled events could cause all or none of the men to eat, or could produce large or small change in attitudes toward eating grasshoppers. Chance factors arising from the testing of subjects in a group could therefore unduly influence the results. Thus, if one popular leader within the group said, "I'll eat a grasshopper. Come on, you guys—what are you, chicken?," we would expect all the men to eat. In short, such a group testing procedure removes the experimental control which is necessary to ensure that the subjects' decision to engage in the discrepant behavior is private. Without proper control we cannot determine whether attitude change is a consequence only of the specified independent variables or of some other factor.

When this study was replicated (as described in the next chapter), some of the subjects were tested in groups, while in other conditions subjects were isolated from other group members. The results for these separated, private subjects were comparable with Smith's group results. They were also similar to other subjects tested at different times in the same study. In contrast, the nonindependent, public decision subjects who were given the same experimental treatments behaved very differently, depending on what happened in their particular group when the request was made to eat the grasshopper. In one group of ten men (in the negative communication condition), one soldier who ate a grasshopper immediately clutched his stomach, yelled out that it tasted like "shit," and pretended to be nauseous. Few others ate, as you might expect, but those who did changed their attitudes very positively. In the other groups given the identical treatment, there was more kidding about the grasshoppers. After one soldier ate a grasshopper and challenged the others to do so, they all ate, but few changed their attitudes of dislike. The data for the first group replicated Smith's results, while that of the second did not. Thus we can see that testing subjects in groups where they can interact with each other can produce uncontrolled results.

Measurement of Attitudes

Initial position artifact. If subjects are *randomly* assigned to different treatment groups, one should expect that their initial attitudes will be comparable *prior* to the introduction of the attitude influence attempt. If there are sizable differences between group means even before they are exposed to the independent variable, then it is impossible to determine whether post-influence behavior is caused by the independent variable alone, or by its interaction with different initial attitudes. On the other hand, if initial rating differences are found, one might look to the experimental situation to see if there were any sources of influence operating *prior* to the initial measurement of attitudes. In the present study, it is obvious that the latter was true. Prior to the first measurement, all men heard what amounted to a brief introductory speech of the purpose of the study. Included in the remarks was a discussion of the need for a mobile army and the need to eat unusual foods, especially survival foods. After having stated that the Quartermaster Corps was sponsoring this research on *food acceptance,* the speech ended with a statement that the experimenter wanted to find out the men's attitudes and reactions to grasshoppers. This is clearly a persuasive communication, the response to which depends largely upon the perceived credibility of the communicator and related situational characteristics (like whether there are others, such as sergeants, nodding in agreement with the statement). It is not surprising, then, that when attitudes were measured just after the initial speech, the ratings of those in the positive communicator condition were more favorable than those in the negative condition. Furthermore, those in the respected leader condition were more favorable toward eating grasshoppers than those in the no influence condition. Both of these effects were greater *before* the manipulation of the independent variables than *after* it!

Sensitization and guinea pig effects. If subjects know that an experimenter is concerned solely with their attitudes toward a single object, and perceive that there is an attempt to change that attitude, how might they act? At one extreme, some subjects may give the experimenter what they think he wants to find, regardless of their true attitudes. At the other extreme, they may resent being guinea pigs and openly resist any change in the direction advocated. Because of this, researchers in attitude change try to disguise both the purpose of their study and the independent variable being assessed for its persuasibility. They also attempt to minimize the salience of the particular attitude selected for modification.

In the present study it was very likely that some subjects perceived a *manipulative intent* on the part of the experimenter. This possibility is enhanced by the procedure that was used. The subject was first told that the experiment concerned attitudes and reactions to grasshoppers and was asked for his current attitude. He was then asked to eat a grasshopper and, finally, to state his "new" attitude. Each person was given a three-page questionnaire and was told to indicate his initial attitude toward only one thing—grasshoppers—on the first page. He held on to this questionnaire while the induction took place (without opening it?) and then put his post-attitude rating in the same booklet. The subject is clearly sensitized to the food to be eaten, which is made highly salient, and he is also sensitized to the fact that the experimenter is interested in whether attitudes toward grasshoppers *change* after exposure to them. Thus attitude change may be a function of (a) the subject's willingness to comply with the apparent purpose of the experiment, (b) the tendency to resist the experimenter's attempt to manipulate and make guinea pigs of the subjects, or (c) a combination of these reactions. When added to the previously noted differences in the *"pre"* ratings, these "guinea pig" effects will simply yield uninterpretable data because of the excessive "error" variance.

One might question the validity of the measurement of liking for the positive and negative communicator on similar grounds. The simple statement to which the men had to respond was a double-barreled item ("friendly and courteous"), loaded to yield a positive response. In addition, it was administered and collected by the same communicator whom each soldier was supposed to be rating.

These considerations, coupled with those raised earlier about the relation of the communicator manipulations to the general Army context, reduce our surprise when we note that *all* subjects rated the communicator as very positive. Where a rating of 7.0 is maximum positiveness, one group averages 6.8 (positive treatment), while the other group averages 6.4 (negative treatment). Even though this mean difference is statistically significant ($p < .01$), can we conclude at a conceptual level that we have a positive and a negative communicator? Or do we only have two levels of a very positive communicator?

Experimental Secrecy

A final point regarding procedure is the problem of maintaining secrecy concerning the experimental manipulations and the purpose of the experiment. Such secrecy is especially warranted when an unusual experiment is conducted in a setting noted for its conventionality and adherence to a standard weekly routine. When the Army reservists were sent back to their unit after participating in this experiment, it seems very unlikely that they would not discuss it in front of, or with, other prospective subjects. There is no indication that experimental subjects were isolated from those about to be tested. The same issue is critical whenever an experiment involves some dramatic aspect, is performed on a captive population where interaction is high, or informs subjects at the conclusion of their testing session of the true purpose and deceptions used in the study. Precautions must be exercised and careful evaluations made of their success, in order to insure that the responses of each subject are not contaminated by prior exposure to previously tested subjects.

RESULTS

Table 4.1 presents the major data from this study. You can now evaluate the validity of the line of reasoning we have advanced in this discussion.

However, throughout this chapter it should be kept in mind that the value of a thorough analysis of an experiment lies in extracting good ideas from less than adequate ways of representing or evaluating them.

TABLE 4.1

Mean Change in Attitudes toward Eating
Grasshoppers and Mean Satisfaction with Group
(Adapted from Smith, 1961a)

Condition	Pretest[1]	Post-test	Attitude change	Satis-faction[2]	Number of ss eating
a) Leader influence	4.6	5.0	+ 0.4	58.0	17/19
b) Humor	2.8	3.6	+ 0.8	49.6	20/20
c) No influence control	3.2	5.1	+ 1.8	62.0	15/17
d) Dissonance, positive communicator	4.0	4.7	+ 0.6	50.7	19/20
e) Dissonance, negative communicator	2.8	5.3	+ 2.5	56.6	10/20

[1] On a 9-point scale where 9.0 is "like extremely," 5.0 is neutral, and 1.0 equals "dislike extremely."

[2] The higher the mean, the more the satisfaction.

An experiment which does not address itself to ideas which are interesting and potentially valuable at either a theoretical or practical level is not worth the effort a critical analysis requires. Those experiments which are interesting and valuable demand that the critic use his evaluation as a basis for concrete suggestions for clarifying the ideas and for testing them appropriately. To criticize for its own sake is to engage in a game of intellectual masturbation with a rather limited and introverted gratification.

COMMUNICATOR CREDIBILITY REVISITED

Of all the conclusions derived from experiments on attitude change, one which is considered to be fairly basic and reliable is Hovland and Weiss' conclusion that a communication is more effective if attributed to a credible source than to a noncredible one. In the previous chapter, this research was described in some detail; let us now reconsider it more critically.

Do the obtained results support the interpretation of communicator credibility? If the data presented in Chapter 3 (in Tables 3.1 and 3.2) are recast as *difference* scores and rearranged in order of most to least attitude change (as in Table 4.2), then we can draw several conclusions that differ from those of Hovland and Weiss.

First, there is additional support for the relationship between trustworthiness and attitude change. In general, as the difference in perceived trustworthiness between communicators increases, the relative effectiveness of the trustworthy communicator also increases. However, to look at the data in another way, large absolute differences in the independent variable

TABLE 4.2

Difference Scores (High Credibility Condition-Low Credibility Condition)
for Percent of Net Attitude Change and for
Percent of Subjects Judging Each Source as Trustworthy[1]
(Adapted from Hovland and Weiss, 1951)

	Issue	Difference Scores for:	
		Net attitude change	Perceived trustworthiness
B.	(Atomic subs)	35.4%	92.4%
A.	(Anti-histamine)	23.4%	88.8%
C.	(Steel shortage)	10.8%	63.9%
D.	(Future of movies)	− 3.3%	68.2%
Average difference		+14.1%	78.2%

[1] The reader should note that the latter is a measure of the subject's interpretation of the independent variable manipulation and not the difference between treatment groups.

(78.2 percent difference in trustworthiness) result in but small differences in the dependent variable (only 14.1 percent difference in attitude change).

It is legitimate, then, to inquire whether this weak effect is significant. It appears from the authors' report that it is *statistically* significant; that is, with the sample size studied (they used 244 observations), and the presumably small variability in response, a difference of 14 percent would occur only three times in one hundred by chance. Thus, we may be reasonably confident in concluding that this is not one of those chance occasions, but rather that this difference is due to the operation of a systematic psychological process which is repeatable under comparable testing conditions. It appears that we are dealing with a variable which has considerable theoretical value for an understanding of how attitudes are influenced by communications.

But can we go one step further and conclude that this finding has practical significance? Can we utilize it and incorporate it into a technology of attitude change? We can, on the one hand, if we simply consider that a difference of 14 percent in a national election would be enough for a candidate to be victorious.

On the other hand, in order to demonstrate a measurable effect upon attitudes, the researchers had to create extreme differences in communicator credibility which, nevertheless, gave only a slight edge to the credible source in producing attitude change. In real life situations, where the naturally existing differences between communicators would be much less extreme, would there still be the same enhancement of the communication by virtue of its attribution to a slightly more credible source? Some of the data suggest that there would not.

One of the positive features of the design of this study is the use of four different attitude issues. If it can be demonstrated that the experimental manipulation had the same effect for all of them, then any conclusions which are drawn are not limited to the content of a particular, arbitrarily chosen, topic. Instead, they are "topic-free" and have a wider range of generalizability. However, this is not the case in the present study, since (as can be seen in Table 4.2) there are different patterns of attitude change for the different topics. The positive relationship between trustworthiness and attitude change is sizable for one issue (B—practicality of atomic subs), moderate for another (A—prescriptions for anti-histamines), but weak and probably not even statistically significant for a third (only 10.8 percent for C—blame for the steel shortage). When we examine the fourth issue used (D—the effect of TV on movies), the generalization breaks down altogether—an untrustworthy communicator is slightly *more* persuasive than a trustworthy one!

We may conclude from this that the relationship is *specific* to the type of issue used, or that only huge differences in trustworthiness lead to meaningful differences in attitude change. Such limitations on this generalization are hard to accept because it is so intuitively reasonable (a more credible communicator *ought* to be more influential). Several lines of inquiry are now open to the reader. He can consider whether the variable of trustworthiness is a major component of credibility, or alternatively, he may question whether the specific operations used in this research to define credibility really tap the essential components of this construct. Another approach is to scrutinize the experimental situation for variables which may have been operating to minimize or distort the effect of credibility on attitude change. Such variables (artifacts) would account for the "slippage" between the big independent variable effect and the small dependent variable result.[2]

THE PROHIBITION CONTROVERSY

Not long ago, a referendum was held in Oklahoma to determine whether its liquor prohibition law would be upheld or repealed. The issue was hotly debated, but the final vote favored prohibition by a narrow margin. Here, then, is an obviously controversial issue on which many people had divergent positions and in which there was considerable personal *involvement*. If you were asked to advise either the Women's Christian Temperance Union (the drys) or liquor distributors (the wets) on tactics to use in this cam-

---

[2] A method for organizing the information in experiments is presented in Postscript D. This outline should aid the reader in these inquiries.

paign, where would you begin? One initial major concern would be the optimal discrepancy between the position represented in your "propaganda" and that of your intended audience. Will a communication be more effective the greater the change it advocates, or is it best to advocate small increments of change?

Obviously, to approach this problem on a trial-and-error basis would be impractical, requiring too much time and money to test out all (or even many) of the possible combinations. What is needed is a general model which interrelates the variables of the audience's initial attitude position, their involvement, and their perception of the communicator's position on the issue. If attitude change could be predicted from a knowledge of the operation of these variables, then one could determine in advance how to design the most effective communication.

An elegant model which appears to fit the bill was in fact proposed by Hovland, Harvey, and Sherif (1957) to help explain the specific problem we have outlined. These investigators maintained that there is a systematic, predictable relationship between a subject's stand on an issue and his perception of the position advocated by a given communicator, and that attitude change is a function of this evaluation of the communicator's position.

Their model can be divided into three processes: the first based upon general judgmental phenomena, the second upon social perception, and the third upon a unique measurement of attitude and its relation to attitude change.

They begin with an unusual point of departure for a model of attitude change—psychophysical studies of weightlifting. The question posed is how the judgments of a series of weights are distorted by the presence of a single weight used as a standard. This "anchor" weight has very different effects upon the subjective judgments of the weights of the series depending upon the relation of its weight to that of the series. If the anchor is much *lighter* than any of the other weights, then the entire series is perceived as heavier than it actually is, while a much *heavier* anchor makes the series appear lighter. In this case, the anchor exerts a *contrast effect* on the judgments of the series. That is, the weights of the series are displaced away from both the anchor and their "true" positions. However, if the weight of the anchor is placed *within* the range of the comparison series, then weights near it will be judged more similar to it than they actually are. That is, weights slightly heavier than the anchor will appear lighter, while slightly lighter ones will appear heavier. This "attraction" exerted by the anchor on the other stimuli is called an *assimilation effect.*

Imagine now this same process of judging an identical series of weights by judges who differed in their experience with handling weights, say a watchmaker and a weightlifter. Their perception of the series would differ if their *experience* served as an "anchor" for their judgments. In fact, it has been demonstrated (by Tresselt, 1948), that watchmakers perceive the weights as heavier, and weightlifters perceive them as lighter than they are.

This basic contrast-assimilation model can be made relevant to our social psychological interests by simply using the subject's *initial attitude* position as the reference anchor against which a series of statements made in a communication is evaluated.

By analogy, this leads to the proposition that in judging the position advocated by a persuasive communicator, the subject's stand on the issue will provide the basis for social contrast or assimilation effects. A communication extremely discrepant from the position of the subject will be seen as more different than it really is (contrasted), while one only slightly discrepant will be seen as more similar to the subject's position (assimilated) than it is in fact.

The final stage in the model is to postulate that the perception of the communicator as divergent results in rejection of his position, and either no attitude change or else a "boomerang" effect (change in direction opposite to that advocated). Perception of the communicator as comparable results in acceptance of his position, and thus positive attitude change.

To make this model testable, it is necessary to define the vague concepts of "slight" and "extreme" discrepancy. This is accomplished by measuring the *verbal structure* of an attitude (rather than by representing attitude as a single point on a given dimension).

The authors measured not only the "most preferred" statement a subject endorsed (about an attitude issue, such as prohibition), but also other statements which he found acceptable (together forming his *latitude of acceptance*). In addition, they assessed those statements which he found objectionable (these formed his *latitude of rejection*). "Slight discrepancy" then refers to those positions discrepant with the recipient's "most acceptable" position but within his latitude of acceptance. "Extreme discrepancy" obviously refers to positions within the latitude of rejection.

We therefore arrive at the prediction that a communication will produce most change if it advocates a position which is at the extreme boundary of a subject's latitude of acceptance, and its effect will be drastically reduced if it falls in the subject's latitude of rejection. This relation holds only when the attitude issue personally involves the subject, because it is only then that his attitude becomes a salient anchor.

To test this model, Hovland, Harvey, and Sherif first determined the latitudes of acceptance and rejection by having subjects evaluate how they felt about each of nine statements which represented the prevailing stands on the issue, ranging from strong advocacy of prohibition to strong advocacy of its repeal. The statements were:

A. Since alcohol is the curse of mankind, the sale and use of alcohol, including light beer, should be completely abolished.

B. Since alcohol is the main cause of corruption in public life, lawlessness, and immoral acts, its sale and use should be prohibited.

C. Since it is hard to stop at a reasonable moderation point in the use of alcohol, it is safer to discourage its use.

D.   Alcohol should not be sold or used except as a remedy for snake bites, cramps, colds, fainting, and other aches and pains.

E.   The arguments in favor of and against the sale and use of alcohol are nearly equal.

F.   The sale of alcohol should be so regulated that it is available in limited quantities for special occasions.

G.   The sale and use of alcohol should be permitted with proper state controls, so that the revenue from taxation may be used for the betterment of schools, highways, and other state institutions.

H.   Since prohibition is a major cause of corruption in public life, lawlessness, immoral acts, and juvenile delinquency, the sale and use of alcohol should be legalized.

I.   It has become evident that man cannot get along without alcohol; therefore, there should be no restriction whatsoever on its sale and use.[3]

An individual's latitude of acceptance is the repertoire of those statements which he says are acceptable, while his latitude of rejection is represented by those positions which he says he finds objectionable. Using each subject's most acceptable position as point of origin (or anchor), it is possible to plot these two scale distances.

This model can then be tested by presenting many communications which advocate each of these nine positions to judges who have a common anchor and therefore equal latitudes of acceptance-rejection. This is more difficult than the alternative approach actually employed by the investigators. They presented one communication (at a fixed position) to judges whose own positions varied along the scale from A to I. This latter technique, incidentally, was not the one these investigators first used in deriving their model from weight judgments.

Strong empirical support for the theoretically predicted, complex assimilation-contrast function appears to come from the data presented in the graph below (Figure 4.1).

A tape-recorded fifteen-minute communication advocating a moderately wet position (position F) was evaluated by subjects whose own most acceptable position varied from A (extreme dry) to H (very wet; no extreme wets could be found). Plotted on the graph are two sets of data. On the ordinate is the perception of the *communication* by subjects whose own true position (represented on the abscissa) is from A to H. The second set of data is the perception of the communication by the same subjects according to their *mean acceptable* position. The solid line represents the theoretical assimilation-contrast curve which the researchers believe best fits their ob-

---

[3] These statements are not as equally spaced as they might seem, since they were not derived from Thurstone's "equal-appearing interval" scale (see Postscript A). The order of the items was arbitrarily arranged by the experimenters.

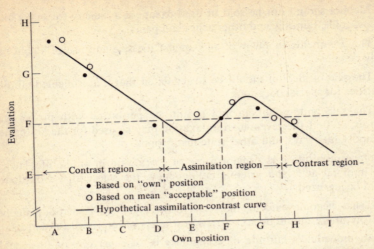

Figure 4.1 Average placement of position of moderately wet communication by subjects holding various positions on the issue, with superimposed hypothetical assimilation-contrast curve (from Hovland, Harvey, and Sherif, 1957).

tained data. If there was no effect of the subject's own position (his anchor) on the perception of the position advocated by the communication, then a horizontal line drawn through position F (the true position of the communication) across the entire graph would depict such a lack of interrelationship. Here we seem to be viewing one of the rare instances in psychology where a complex prediction, generated by a simple model, of a function which changes direction (i.e., is nonmonotonic) is verified by data.

But are we examining judgmental distortion phenomena or merely an illusion? When subjected to critical analysis, this dramatic effect vanishes. We first eliminate one of the two sets of data since they are not independent (i.e., a "mean acceptable" data point includes the ratings of subjects who are also represented at the adjacent "own position" data points). We then equate the size of the scale units used on the two axes (the ordinate is justifiably stretched to magnify the effect). Finally, by taking away the theoretical curve, we remove the "guiding influence" exerted upon our perception of the data. What remains is the graph in Figure 4.2.

A horizontal ("no effect") line best fits all but two data points. Thus there is support for a contrast effect only when extreme drys respond to a moderately discrepant communication. But before we draw this conclusion, let us reexamine the nature of the subjects who are represented by these two data points.

The drys at positions A and B are those who endorse the extreme statements that alcohol is the "curse of mankind," and the "cause of cor-

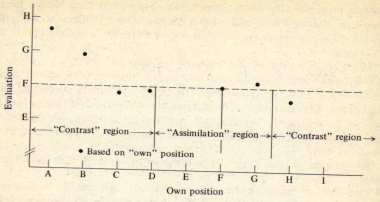

Figure 4.2 Same data as in Fig. 4.1, with the following changes: "Evalua-tion" axis is equated with "Own position" axis, data based on mean "accept-able" position is excluded, and hypothetical assimilation-contrast curve is excluded (adapted from Hovland, Harvey, and Sherif, 1957).

ruption in public life, lawlessness, and immoral acts." Clearly then, such attitudes toward drinking reflect a pervasive underlying value structure centering about human dignity, loss of control, law and order, and sin. From what population do these subjects come? "The dry group selection was relatively easy," according to the investigators. 183 subjects from the Women's Christian Temperance Union, the Salvation Army, and ministry student groups were used. These people are members of groups seriously concerned about drinking and its anti-social consequences. This is compar-able to using Boy Scouts when studying attitudes toward camping, or Black Panther members when the attitude dimension is black self-reliance and dignity.

A number of conceptual problems immediately become apparent when we note that in this experiment such naturally existing groups are being compared with other subjects drawn from very different populations. The wets were composed of forty-one people personally known to the research team (faculty colleagues, graduate students, liquor salesmen?) and 290 middle-of-the-road undergraduates.

Thus attitudes toward prohibition differ not only in extremity among these groups but also, more importantly, in their intrinsic relation to the self-definition of the WCTU members and to the very core of their group's purpose in being. To change such an attitude is to destroy the group and to reorganize a complex system of the personal values of its constituents. Attitudes toward drinking and prohibition ought to be highly correlated for such groups. However, consider a group of liquor distributors. Their attitude toward prohibition might reflect only its instrumental relation to a more general attitude of making money. They would be for repeal of prohibition if selling liquor legally would gain them money, but they would be *for* prohibition if they could make more money selling it illegally. Thus the basis for their involvement in the issue is on a different level than that of the WCTU ladies.

There could be differences between the wets and the drys in education and intelligence which would affect the comprehension of the communication, or the sophistication necessary to critically evaluate persuasive communications. There could also be differences in the specific training people have had to defend the relevant group norm. In addition, the immediate social support for the drys' initial attitude position (if the WCTU and Salvation Army were tested in identifiable groups) would be much higher than for the wets (since the wets had nothing to make them identifiable as a group).

This line of reasoning raises the question suggested in Postscript B as the experimenter's dilemma: should he maximize the impact of the independent variable by the use of its naturally existing manifestations (thereby losing much control and analytical precision), or should he sacrifice its impact by use of experimentally created variables (which allow a better conceptualization of the processes and causal relations involved)? Furthermore, selection of subjects active in groups which publicly advocate a given stand on the issue in question has been suggested as the best technique for studying and manipulating the variable of "ego-involvement." Certainly such a strategy yields groups with more intense levels of involvement, but the natural selection of an independent variable always means that there is a host of factors correlated with its presence. Many of these factors may be unknown, yet may in fact be producing the observed effect on the behavior. Once you know that subjects in a high-involvement group change their attitudes less in a response to a communication than subjects in a low-involvement group, how do you interpret the finding? Natural differences in involvement might reflect differences in public commitment, prior effort expended, available social support, information about the issue, special characteristics of group membership, costs of maintaining group membership, sensitivity to attacks on the group or the subject's attitude position, suspicion of manipulative intent, experience in counterarguing, and who knows what else?

While we want a powerful, natural manipulation, it is only with skillfully created experimental designs and strategies, and carefully controlled manipulations to guide the digging and sifting operations, that an experiment will provide the interpretative clarity we must demand.

ROLE-PLAYING AND IMPROVISATION AS CHANGE TECHNIQUES

A very different goal is advanced by those who use role-playing as a technique for producing changes in attitude. Here the desired changes are often subtle modifications of a person's perception and evaluation of another (usually someone he dislikes). A related goal is to make the person more tolerant of a given contrary position by having him publicly espouse a set of opinions with which he strongly disagrees.

The conclusion derived from this body of research is considered to be the most reliable in the area of attitude change: Active participation is more effective in changing attitudes than is passive exposure to persuasive communications.

Although the studies vary considerably in the form of role-playing utilized (from debate to psychodrama), they share the minimal requirement of the technique, which is that the subject become involved in the attempt to present, sincerely and convincingly, the attitude position of another person.

The self-persuasion which occurs as a consequence of effective role-playing is also interesting because it does not fit the traditional attitude-change model. The change in attitude is the result of a person's communication to *himself* of a counter-norm position.

One of the few systematic attempts to explore the variables in role-playing which influence attitude change has been the series of studies by Janis and King, previously described in Chapter 3. The reader will remember that these investigators attempted to understand their earlier empirical finding (that "overt verbalization induced through role-playing tends to augment the effectiveness of a persuasive communication") by isolating the variable of *improvisation* from that of *satisfaction* as the major determinant in the acceptance of new ideas.

The data in Table 4.3 led them to conclude that subjects who were required to improvise a speech contrary to their own position adjusted their attitudes to conform with their role behavior more than did subjects who were required to read a prepared speech opposing their own position. This result occurred even though both the improvised and prepared speeches contained similar arguments and conclusions.

If the reader examines the values of net opinion change for each of the five items, and also notes the meaning of the *combined index* of change, it becomes clear that two conclusions, rather than only one, are warranted by these data. Improvisation *is* more effective than the other treatments on items 1, 2, and 3, but it is *not* on items 4 and 5. These two clusters of items differ in the degree to which they are informationally and factually based (1 to 3), or self-relevant (4, 5). Other research in this area has also failed to find a significant effect of improvisation on attitude change when the opinions measured were self-descriptions of the subject's expectations or feelings. Thus, the authors' general conclusion must be limited to one class of opinion items. However, it is reasonable to presume that there may be a two-stage process in which a person first intellectually incorporates new information into his repertoire of verbal responses, and then subsequently accepts it at a personal level. In the brief time span used in the present study, only the first stage of this process may have been revealed by the measurements.

TABLE 4.3

Net Change in Opinions Related to Exposure and Improvisation
(Adapted from King and Janis, 1956)

	Exposure:	Active		Passive
	Improvise:	Yes %	No %	Silent read %
1. Estimate of required length of service for draftees		41	27	5
2. Estimates of college students' chances of being deferred		44	26	25
3. Estimates of college students' chances of becoming officers		70	47	45
4. Expectations concerning the length of *one's own* military service if drafted		59	46	50
5. Expectations concerning the length of one's own deferment before being drafted		50	26	55
Combined index: percentage influenced on three or more of the five opinion items		87.5	54.5	65

*p-value = .01   **p-value = .03

This analysis highlights a source of confusion for many students of the behavioral sciences, namely, that apparent contradictions between conclusions are often due to comparing the authors' generalizations instead of directly comparing the data across the studies in dispute.

What about the satisfaction explanation? Is there any evidence that active participation has its effect because those subjects are more satisfied with their performance? The evidence clearly refutes this alternative. Subjects in the nonimprovisation condition rated themselves as more satisfied with their performance than did those in the improvisation condition, but they changed their attitudes less. In the nonimprovisation group, 96 percent of the subjects felt that their "performance was at least satisfactory," while only 63 percent of those in the improvisation group felt satisfied (a very significant difference of 33 percent, $p < .01$).

But this is only an indirect way of ruling out the "satisfaction hypothesis." Rather than basing conclusions on correlational data, a better strategy would be if "the experimenter differentially administered social rewards and punishments for the purpose of varying the satisfaction variable under conditions in which improvisation was held constant." (p. 182)

This is exactly what these investigators did, by randomly dividing the subjects within the improvisation group into three equal subgroups. Subjects received either positive, negative, or no evaluative feedback after their speech. This manipulation had the expected significant effect of altering self-ratings of satisfaction, but had no effect upon attitude change (p. 182).

While this finding convincingly eliminates satisfaction as a reasonable hypothetical process in this particular attitude change paradigm, it raises two problems of interpretation, one of internal validity and one of external validity. Remember that one-third of the subjects in the improvisation condition were told that they did not improvise well. If this manipulation of satisfaction had been successful, it should have made about 33 percent of the subjects in the improvisation group feel that their performance was not "at least satisfactory." This is precisely the difference previously reported between the *entire* improvisation and nonimprovisation groups. Put differently, 33 percent fewer subjects in the improvisation condition were satisfied than in the nonimprovisation condition, *not* because they had to improvise, but because the experimenter told 33 percent of the subjects that their performance was not satisfactory.

The question of how these results compare to other established findings in psychology (external validity) comes to the fore when we note that reward and punishment (the feedback manipulations) following a behavior (emitting counter-norm statements) had no subsequent effect upon that behavior—or at least upon accepting those statements—contrary to basic principles of reinforcement.

The final point we would like to note is the active vs. passive exposure effect. These investigators, although primarily interested in the variable of improvisation, nevertheless include in their design a *systematic replication* of the conditions for retesting the active participation main effect they established in their previous study.[4]

However, if the reader re-examines Table 4.3, he may be surprised to see that the basic finding, the superiority of active over passive exposure, is *not* found. Indeed, silent reading is slightly more effective in changing attitudes than active participation which involves public reading. To explain such a result, we could look to the specific conditions of testing used in this study. These may have introduced variables not present in previous studies which changed the expected main effect. For example, it may have been that the instructions given the public reading subjects (nonimprovisation treatment) focused their attention on the *mechanics* of speech delivery rather than on the *content* of their speech. The passive controls might have been attending more to the content, since public speaking was not of concern to them. On the other hand, improvisation subjects would have to be

---

[4] This desirable feature ensures that the basic conditions for demonstrating the over-all effect have been established with the particular setting, subjects, manipulations, and measurements used. Upon this baseline, analyses of the components, processes, and interactions of old with new variables can be made more confidently.

interested in the content, since they had to generate it, as well as in its mode of delivery. *Post hoc* analyses such as this are of value if they correctly direct us to hitherto unsuspected sources of variability in our procedures, or if they lead to explicit hypotheses which are then tested in new experiments.

To conclude the analysis of this experiment on an optimistic note, it might be said that improvisation was in fact more effective than it appears from the data presented. If the essential ingredient in improvised role-playing is "sincerely advocating the role," then attitude change should be greatest for those subjects in the improvisation condition who did role-play sincerely. In the present study only 47 percent felt that they gave the "impression of being 'sincere.' " This is important because the experimental demand "to improvise" will be met very differently by individual subjects according to their intelligence, verbal fluency, shyness, experience with the issue, argumentativeness, preparation time, and other variables. The importance of creating experimental conditions which make improvisation more probable is emphasized by Jansen and Stolurow (1962): "the relative ineffectiveness of improvisation might be explained by the fact that improvising is not an activity which can be done on request, but has to be developed with great care and can be expected to appear only after careful preparation." (p. 22)

SCIENTIFIC METHOD REQUIRES CONSTRUCTIVE CRITICISM

By now it should be apparent to the reader that there should never be uncritical acceptance of the conclusion of any experiment. One of the virtues of the scientific method (which is the substructure upon which all experimental approaches rest) is its creation in the scientific community of attitudes of open-mindedness toward one's own work, of responsiveness to constructive criticism, and of the provisional nature of all "truth."

We have applied a critical approach to several studies in order to reveal to the student the level of concern and attention he must bring to a serious evaluation of any scientifically gathered evidence. In so doing, we have tried to illustrate some general problems of methodology, subject selection, data analysis, and presentation, as well as of theoretical interpretation. However, the fact that such problems exist in these studies does not mean that they should be dismissed. Our guiding principle is that the only experiments worth such a thorough, critical evaluation are those which contain ideas of potential theoretical or practical value. A trivial idea does not merit the time and effort required in applying the kind of critical approach that we have demonstrated in this chapter. Such a value judgment, of course, demands that the student first become acquainted with the basic issues in the area under consideration.

ATTITUDE MEASUREMENT: TO EACH HIS OWN

Analysis at the level of the single experiment must be supplemented by analysis of a series of related experiments in a given area. There are problems which become apparent only when we have accumulated enough knowledge in a field of inquiry to be able to step back and take a broader view of the entire body of research in that area. Critical analysis must be applied to the assumptions, strategies, definitions, manipulations, and measurement across comparable studies, as well as within each study.

In making comparisons across studies, we note one glaring fact—the lack of common methods for measuring attitudes, and a similar confusion regarding the definition of attitudes. To illustrate the chaos which can result from failure to adopt common standards, we need only outline the variety of measures used to define attitude change. There are two parts to this problem; first, the subject's response task may be markedly different from one study to another, and second, even when they are identical, the experiments may use different techniques of translating these common responses into quantitatively derived dependent variables. An example of the latter problem can be seen when two studies ask the subject to give his opinion by checking one point along a pro-con, like-dislike scale. Attitude change may then be described in terms of any one of the following measures: (a) percent subjects showing any positive change at all, (b) percent subjects showing "large," "moderate," "small" or "no" change (categories arbitrarily defined), (c) net percent change (positive minus negative changes), (d) any of the above for an arbitrarily determined combination of opinion items, (e) the absolute mean scale distance changed, (f) distance changed relative to amount of change possible, and (g) scale distance change weighted (corrected) for the subjective distance between scale points (i.e., two units movement across neutral is "worth more" than two units within one side of the scale.)

The *a priori* rating scales which have been used have varied in the number of scale points (from four to one hundred), in the presence and number of verbal labels at various points, and in their arrangement (horizontal or vertical).

Attitudes have been measured by scale ratings of verbal statements (agree-disagree, true-false, like-dislike, etc.), of objects (good-bad, desirable-undesirable), of other people (like-dislike), and of self (degree of esteem, confidence). They have been measured by ratings of acceptance and rejection of individual opinion statements (latitudes of acceptance-rejection) and by choices, ranking of alternatives, perceived instrumental value of items or actions, ratings of mood, ratings of intention, willingness to endorse an action or product, and likelihood of future behavior.

Behavioral, or nonquestionnaire (non-paper-and-pencil), measures of attitude have also included an impressively divergent array. Verbal reports (about smoking, serving certain foods, dental hygiene practices) have been used, as well as observations of actual compliance with recommendations (taking an X-ray, getting tetanus shots, eating, agreeing with group norm, etc.). Time measures (decision time, time spent listening to supportive information, etc.), physiological measures (galvanic skin response to indicate reactions of a prejudiced person to stimuli associated with minority groups), and learning measures (recall of stimuli) have all been conceived of as indicators of attitude. There are many others which rely on unobtrusive observational methods (e.g., a count of empty beer and whiskey bottles in the garbage cans, as indicative of attitudes toward liquor in a given neighborhood; druggists' records of which doctors prescribe new drugs; the seating pattern of black and white students in classrooms and cafeterias).

Two additional comments about attitude measurement deserve to be made. First, while attitudes are sometimes defined as being composed of at least two components, cognitive and affective, what is traditionally done in attitude change studies is to present a set of belief or cognitive statements in a communication, and to then measure only changes in affect. Even more curious is the paradox of two seemingly interdependent areas of investigation—psychological scaling (psychometrics) and attitude change—existing independently and even in ignorance of each other. Few of the hundreds of studies performed on attitude change make use of the scaling techniques developed by Thurstone, Likert, Guttman, Osgood, Coombs, Lazarsfeld and others (see Postscript A for a survey of some of these). On the other hand, it is equally rare for those interested in measurement and scaling procedures to be concerned with the use of their techniques as part of an empirical study of communication and attitude change (Osgood's use of the semantic differential is a notable exception).

The lack of a common definition of attitude, or of what constitutes a valid and reliable measurement of it, is similarly reflected in the failure to use comparable attitude topics, communciations with similar structure, or even standardized manipulations of the independent variables (e.g., refer to Chapter 3 for the different operations used to define the variable of "distraction").

Having seen the great variety of measures (operational definitions) employed for attitudes, it is no longer surprising that results in this area often conflict. The experimenters who use the various measures of attitude often make their decisions on the basis of ease of measurement, or intuition. There is often no theoretical reason why the measurements used *should* be measuring the same thing. It is merely assumed that they do. Since the results from various experiments sometimes conflict, we are left with the conclusion that the measures probably do not measure the same thing.

If attitude measurement is in such a state of confusion, what can we who are interested in producing large and lasting changes in attitudes do with the results of these experiments? Where do we go from here?

CHAPTER FIVE

Reflecting on the Role of Theory in Attitude Change

For the person who is looking for techniques to produce attitude and behavior change, the previous chapter concluded with what seemed to be a
real problem. Researchers who claim to be working with the same conceptual variable, namely attitude change, use an array of what appear to be
inconsistent methods. There appears to be little agreement among them as
to what constitutes a *reasonable* measure of attitudes or a *reasonable* opera-
tionalization of the most commonly studied conceptual independent variables. If it were possible to determine why such differences exist in definition and procedures, it should also be possible to determine how to use the
results of these seemingly inconsistent experiments to the best advantage in
devising techniques for producing change.

WHY INCONSISTENCY IN DEFINING ATTITUDES?

In thinking about how to conceptually define an attitude, experimenters
often use their own *intuitive* notions about what attitudes are. Typically,
these notions or ideas are not *explicitly* stated by the experimenter, but are
derived from what he believes to be a reasonable operational definition of
attitudes. He usually does the same thing for the independent variables in
which he is interested. Since the intricacies of the experimenter's concept of
what he means by a specific attitude are often left implicit, it is not sur-

prising that other researchers come up with slightly different concepts and therefore different operations for the "same" conceptual variable. Thus one reason why there is such a proliferation of operations for what are labelled "attitudes" is because these researchers' concepts of "attitude" are, in fact, different. Furthermore, these differences are not always apparent.

A second reason for the inconsistency in measurement of attitudes, even though some researchers do have the same conceptual definition of attitudes, is that they use *different* rules for deriving a reasonable operation of the *same* conceptual variable. That is, two researchers who agree on the concept of an attitude may disagree (although, again, usually implicitly) on what is the best method for deriving an operation of the concept. For example, they might feel that affect is a crucial aspect of all attitudes; however, one researcher might use logic to derive his operation of affect, while the other might use "intuition."

Unfortunately, such inconsistency in defining concepts and in setting up *correspondence rules* (rules which allow an experimenter to make a correspondence between a specific operation and a conceptual variable) has led to a great deal of what seem to be inconsistent, and therefore trivial, results from a number of experiments.

Faced with the problem of inconsistent conceptual definitions and correspondence rules, what can be done to salvage the experiments already conducted and to direct future research so that similar problems do not reoccur? There are three possible techniques we might use to insure standardization. The first (and most obvious) is to design experiments which control as many sources of bias as possible. Some of the more sophisticated experimental designs which have been devised especially for this purpose are presented in Postscript C.

The two remaining techniques for solving these problems are: (1) to develop a *theory* which makes explicit the definitions of relevant conceptual variables, as well as the correspondence rules, and (2) to accept the inconsistency found between results of different experiments as psychologically valid, and then to determine how that inconsistency can direct us in reconceptualizing the variables that control human behavior. The remainder of this chapter is an extension and evaluation of each of these two solutions.

WHAT ARE THEORIES?

Essentially, a theory is an abstract, symbolic representation of what is conceived to be reality. That is, a theory is a set of abstract statements or rules which are designed to "fit" some portion of the real world. A model airplane is, in some sense, a concrete theory of a real airplane. We can use the model plane to test how a real airplane will behave (fly) under various conditions, if we assume that the model "fits" with the real plane. If we subject the model airplane to certain air currents (as in a wind tunnel) and observe how it behaves, we should be able to predict from its behavior the behavior of a real plane subjected to similar air currents. The accuracy of our predictions (or hypotheses) will be a function of how well the model "fits," or represents, the real plane.

In the same way that the model is used to predict the behavior of the real plane, a set of symbolic statements could be created to do the same thing. In order to use a theory (set of symbolic statements) to predict behavior, we need two sets of rules. One set of rules has to relate some of the symbols (called conceptual independent variables) in our theory to aspects of the air current, while other symbols in the theory (called conceptual dependent variables) have to relate to the behavior of the real airplane. These are the correspondence rules. The other set of rules must tell us how to manipulate the symbols or concepts of the theory so that we can derive the necessary hypotheses. In physical science theories, these rules are typically mathematical ones, or rules of abstract algebra and calculus. That is, if the symbol X represents some change in air current, and Y the initial position of the airplane before the change in air current, then the rule given for predicting the effect which the change in current will have on the behavior of the plane might be: $Y \times X =$ new position. Our rule here is: multiply X and Y to get the new position of the plane. Theories need not use *only* mathematical rules to tell us how to derive the effect that a conceptual independent variable will have on a conceptual dependent variable. In fact, most theories in psychology use rules of grammar and implicit semantics to suggest how to manipulate these symbols.

In summary, a theory is merely an abstract way of relating some events in the world. It should give the experimenter correspondence rules for relating conceptual variables to specific operations. It should also tell the experimenter how to manipulate and interrelate the various conceptual variables. Once they are so related, the experimenter can (deductively) derive specific hypotheses of an "if . . . then" sort. If a certain value of the independent variable occurs (e.g., wind current) then the dependent variable should be affected in a given way (e.g., the airplane's movement should change a given amount). Theories also incorporate a number of *hypothetical* variables and assumptions whose sole purpose is to relate the conceptual variables to each other. They are not directly related to operations, but rather to other conceptual variables which are themselves tied to specific operations. It follows, therefore, that these hypothetical variables can be validated only indirectly, even when the entire theory is supported by sound evidence.

HOW IS A THEORY USEFUL?

A theory makes explicit what is meant by a conceptual variable. By allowing only certain correspondence rules, a theory limits the operations which can be used for a particular conceptual variable, and makes explicit what those operations must be. Furthermore, a theory, by using a set of rules and hypothetical constructs to relate conceptual variables, allows the experimenter to derive *new* relationships. That is, a theory suggests how events in the world (operations) ought to be related even *before* these events have been observed. For example, the movements of the known planets led astronomers to predict that there must be another planet at a given distance from the sun. This theoretically guided search subsequently uncovered the existence of the plant Uranus.

When an experimental test of a prediction is validated, then the entire theory from which it was derived receives support. In addition, this new empirical finding is related by the theory to a body of previously established results. Theories thus help to formulate a network of interrelated facts and principles which explain some portion of reality.

In summary, theories are vital in any systematic approach to understanding complex phenomena because:

a)   they can generate predictions about complex functional relationships between variables (not merely all-or-none or simple monotonic functions);

b)   they integrate many empirical observations which, on the surface, may appear to be dissimilar;

c)   they separate relevant from irrelevant variables, and provide schema for organizing the relevant ones;

d)   they allow for the derivation of nonobvious predictions (i.e., statements about reality which one would not make on the basis of intuition);

e)   they explain why variables function as they do, often by postulating hypothetical processes.

In psychology, theories are designed to relate changes in stimulus conditions to changes in the behavior of humans and animals, just as the theory of aerodynamics tries to relate changes in air currents to changes in the behavior of a plane or rocketship. Theories of attitude change also try to relate stimulus conditions and organismic variables to observed changes in verbal and nonverbal behavior via the central conceptual variable of attitude change, as well as by a number of intermediary processes.

But there are relatively few explicitly stated theories of attitude change (see Insko, 1967, for a survey of all existing theories). Why should this be so, if theories offer so many advantages? The simplest explanation for the absence of theory in this area (and indeed, in most areas of social psychology) is that building a theory which accounts for complex behavior is the most difficult of all intellectual activities. Not only does it require an unusual level of creative ability, but it demands other attributes of the theory builder. He must have the *chutzpah* (daring, confidence, effrontery) to risk being wrong when he offers his simplified view of reality. Built into any good theory is a method of proof which will allow the possibility of the theory being disproven. In fact, much of the research which a theory stimulates is designed to prove it wrong, in part or completely. Thus while this intellectual activity may yield large rewards, the likelihood of failure is even greater.

What happens when a theory is not supported by a test of its predictions? At first, the theory is modified to accommodate the inconsistent evidence. But as the inconsistent evidence mounts, too many additional assumptions are required. The theory then begins to lose its virtue of parsimony, that of providing a brief explanation for a large variety of phenomena. It may be a difficult task to construct a theory, but it is even more difficult to scrap one that is wrong, once it is in use. Conant (1951), after reviewing many theories (e.g., of combustion and of the solar system), concluded that a theory is never overthrown by contradictory data; it is only cast aside when a superior theory replaces it. Therefore, a bad theory not only outlives its usefulness, but it may also delay adequate testing and acceptance of better theories.

There is no question but that the field of attitude change needs an adequate theory to organize, integrate, and explain what has been found already; to resolve the many existing empirical discrepancies; and to guide the search for new techniques and methods of producing and measuring attitude change. It is equally clear, however, that we must critically evaluate any proposed theory, lest the need for theory foster premature acceptance of a less than satisfactory one.

Of the possible theories we might present, we have chosen the one which has stimulated the most research (over 300 studies in ten years) and also the most controversy. In addition, it postulates an interesting approach to changing attitudes which differs from all competing theories.

COGNITIVE DISSONANCE THEORY

Cognitive dissonance theory, which was formulated by Leon Festinger in 1957, is based on a few main assumptions about how the human organism works. The central assumption is that human beings cannot tolerate inconsistency. This means that whenever inconsistency exists in a person, he will try to eliminate or reduce it. There are, of course, many kinds of inconsistency, but the theory of cognitive dissonance only applies to *psychological* inconsistency (in which, by the way, may be included logical inconsistency). When psychological inconsistency exists, it does two things to the organism: it activates him and it directs him. The inconsistency thus pushes (motivates) the organism in a specific direction which, if acted upon, will result in reduction of the unpleasant tension produced by the inconsistency.

The theory states that dissonance (psychological inconsistency) exists whenever one cognitive element conflicts with (is dissonant with) another cognitive element. These cognitive elements are bits of knowledge (it is raining), or opinions (I like the rain), or beliefs (the rain makes flowers grow), either about the environment or about oneself. In order for dissonance to exist, one cognitive element must be about oneself. Let's look at some examples. A soldier in Vietnam would have the following cognition about himself, "I am fighting in the American army in Vietnam." Suppose this soldier was also against the war in Vietnam; he would then have the opinion, "I am against the war in Vietnam." These two cognitive elements do not follow from each other; they are in fact dissonant. If the soldier is against the war, he feels he ought not to be fighting in it. Another example deals with smoking. Smokers have the cognition, "I smoke." The knowledge (which a smoker may have) of the evidence which ties smoking to lung cancer is dissonant with the knowledge that he smokes. That is, if smoking causes lung cancer, he feels he ought not to smoke. These examples should demonstrate what is meant by cognitive elements, and also by dissonance existing between discrepant cognitive elements.

Cognitive elements can be in one of three relationships: dissonant, consonant, and irrelevant. In the Vietnam War example, a consonant element with, "I am against the war," would be, "I may be in the army, but I never shoot my gun at North Vietnamese." A cognitive element which is irrelevant would be, "I smoke." When considering the cognitive elements which have been presented, it should be noted that some of the elements are linked to the person's behavior and others to the environment. This implies that changes in the environment and in the person's behavior will produce changes in the cognitive elements of our subject. If our subject stopped smoking, the cognitive element, "I smoke," would obviously change to, "I don't smoke." Thus a crucial point in the theory is that one of the ways in which our subject can change a set of dissonant cognitive elements to a set of consonant elements is by changing his behavior, if that behavior comprises one of the dissonant elements.

To increase its predictive power, the theory also differentiates between situations producing more or less dissonance. The magnitude of dissonance which the human organism experiences is a function of three conceptual variables. The first of these is the *importance* of each of the cognitive elements. For example, if it weren't important to our hypothetical smoker that he might die of lung cancer (because he was eighty years old and felt he had lived a full life anyway), then there would be little dissonance produced by the two cognitions, "I smoke" and "Smoking is related to lung cancer." On the other hand, the magnitude of the dissonance experienced would be great if our subject did not want to die or become ill.

The second variable which affects the amount of dissonance a person experiences is more difficult to conceptualize. Up to this point, our subject has been walking around with only two or three cognitions in his head. Actually, the human organism knows and believes and has opinions about many things; he has more than two or three cognitions. The magnitude of dissonance a person is experiencing at any one time is therefore a function of the number of dissonant and consonant cognitions which exist at that time. More specifically, the greater the *ratio of dissonant to consonant elements,* the greater the dissonance that is felt. In the previous example of the soldier, there were two cognitions which were dissonant with each other. Adding a third cognition, "I don't shoot the enemy," reduces dissonance by increasing the number of consonant elements. "I don't shoot the enemy" is consonant with "I am against the war." By making dissonance a function of the ratio of dissonant to consonant elements, the theory provides for a dramatic reduction in dissonance merely by the addition of one or two consonant elements.

What may be called *cognitive overlap* also helps determine the amount of experienced dissonance. Cognitive overlap refers to the functional equivalence of the objects or activities represented by each cognition. For example, in a choice between a Volkswagen and a Ford Mustang, the two cars have more features in common than a new car and a new sailboat. That is, there are more cognitive elements functionally similar between two alternatives when they share comparable features. There is less dissonance when one chooses either of the cars than when one chooses the car over the boat, since in the latter decision, many functions served by the boat are not shared by the automobile. Thus the magnitude of dissonance aroused by a decision between alternatives is inversely related to their cognitive overlap (i.e., it is greater, the less they have in common).

Dissonance is more likely to occur in a given situation if the decision-maker *commits* himself to some course of action while remaining aware of his *volition* to do otherwise. These two features of dissonance were added to the original theory by Brehm and Cohen (1962) in order to clarify some predictions from the theory.

Behavioral commitment (public action) is important in the theory for two reasons. First, the observer does not have to make questionable inferences about the person's *covert* decisions, thus permitting more certainty in defining the conditions under which dissonance occurs. Secondly, public action is more anchored in external reality (and "fixed" in time as a fact) than are private responses (thoughts, values, motives, intentions, and attitudes). If resistance to change of a cognitive element is greater when it has an external reality referent than when it corresponds to an internal, subjective state, then the theory can predict which of these two kinds of cognitions will change. The cognition pertaining to overt behavior will not change, and will furthermore exert an influence on subjective states to make them agree with the overt behavior.

This last point raises the crucial issue of the importance of dissonance *reduction* in the theory. Once dissonance is aroused, there will be a *need* to reduce dissonance. This need to reduce the psychological tension created by inconsistency motivates a wide variety of behavior. It is only by observing the presence and characteristics of dissonance-reducing behavior that one can infer that dissonance must have been present. This is to say that since dissonance and magnitude of dissonance are hypothetical states, there is no direct, independent metric of them. Rather, they can be inferred only from the antecedent conditons which *ought* (by theoretical definition) to generate dissonance, or from the theoretically derived consequences of what should happen if dissonance were present.

Dissonance may be reduced in many ways: (a) by attempting to revoke the decision, (b) by lowering the importance of the cognitions or the decision, (c) by increasing the cognitive overlap between cognitive elements (searching for or misperceiving aspects of functional equivalence), and (d) by adding consonant elements to change the ratio of dissonant to consonant ones.

To illustrate how these techniques might be employed in a simple example, imagine a professor who, after much mental conflict, gives up a position at one college for a position at another. There are many good features of his old college which he loses in going to the new one, and a number of negative features of the new one which he inherits by his choice. These two sets of cognitions contain elements which introduce dissonance following his decision to change colleges. He can then attempt to reduce his dissonance in several ways:

a)   By either seeing the new job as only temporary, or by actually allowing himself to be persuaded back to his old job or to a third alternative;

b)   By changing his evaluation of the importance of those positive features of the old college and the negative features of the new (e.g., it does not matter if the old college has more intelligent students; lack of research facilities at the new college is not so important because he can spend more time doing neglected library research);

c)   By minimizing the differences between the ability of his colleagues at the two schools, between the faculty clubs, etc.;

d)   By seeking out colleagues who like being at the new college and those who have also left the old one, or finding unexpected virtues related to being at the new college (like the availability of good delicatessens).

There are two classes of decision-making situations which the theory describes as areas of relevant application: forced public compliance and free-choice decision-making.

An example of the first might occur when a student who is *against* police interference on academic campuses is required to give a speech in his speech class in *favor* of police interference. When the student gives a speech against his own position, dissonance is aroused. However, the student would experience greater dissonance if he volunteered to give the speech than if he gave it to avoid receiving an F in the course. Dissonance could be reduced, in this instance, by the student changing his attitude toward police interference in the direction of the speech he was making, or by denying he made the speech, or by adding his own reasons to justify his act of public compliance. The amount of dissonance which will be experienced in a forced-compliance situation, and therefore the magnitude of the pressure to reduce dissonance, is an inverse function of the justification for engaging in the compliant behavior.

Of course, not all situations which confront humans force the organism to comply to some demands. Some situations involve free choice. However, dissonance can also be produced in these instances. In the forced-compliance situation, the greater the magnitude of initial justification, the *less* the amount of dissonance experienced. In a free-choice situation, justification is also an important variable but in a slightly different sense. In making a choice between buying one of two record albums (perhaps a more relevant example than that of the professor's choice), there are usually positive and negative aspects associated with each album. For example, one album may have great songs, but the group singing them might not be good, while the opposite may be true of the other album. A choice is always a potentially dissonance-producing situation. After one album is chosen, the loss of the *positive* qualities of the unchosen album is dissonant with the knowledge that that album was not chosen. Specifically, if the album with good songs is chosen, then two cognitions which are dissonant are, "I like the group which sings on album A," and "I have chosen album B." It does not follow that album B should be chosen if album A has the preferred group. However, choosing album B is consonant with the fact that album B has the better songs. It is possible to derive the following prediction about justification from the above analysis. More dissonance should exist *after* the decision is made if the two alternatives are nearly equally attractive. That is, the less justification (the fewer reasons) one has for choosing one or the other alternative, the greater the dissonance. In this case, justification involves the difference in initial attractiveness of the two alternatives in the choice. For example, if one album is clearly superior in all respects to another, then choosing it produces very little dissonance.

When dissonance is produced following a choice, the main method of dissonance reduction is *increasing* the attractiveness of the chosen alternative and *decreasing* the attractiveness of the unchosen alternative. In the record album example, the album which is chosen will be seen as more and more attractive. The subject may claim that not only are the songs better, but he was tired of the other group and had too many of its records already.

Until the music-lover completes this difficult choice, he is in a state of conflict. It is only after one album is chosen that dissonance (which is a *post-decisional* phenomenon) must be considered if we are to understand the changes in perception, attitude, and behavior which will follow. To review:

1.   Dissonance is always aroused by the discrepancy between two or more relevant cognitive elements, when one is about a person's behavior (his choice or compliant act) and the other is about his internal or external environment.

2.   The magnitude of dissonance is a function of the ratio of dissonant to consonant elements, the importance of these elements, and the cognitive overlap between them. The initial amount of dissonance will be a function of the number of reasons (consonant elements) for either complying to external demands, or choosing one alternative over another.

3.   The greater the initial magnitude of dissonance, the greater will be the drive to reduce dissonance by changing one or more of the dissonant cognitive elements or by adding new consonant elements.

4.   A person can reduce dissonance either by changing his behavior, or by changing his internal environment (attitudes and perceptions) or his external environment.

A SAMPLE OF EXPERIMENTS DERIVED FROM DISSONANCE THEORY

To understand how the theory works, we must examine various attempts to test derivations from it. The examples we have selected from the many available deal with changes in different kinds of attitudes: toward objects, toward activities, toward groups, and toward self. Moreover, we have tried to illustrate interesting general features of theoretically guided research, as well as the cumulative development and refinement of ideas which good theory-testing encourages.

AN IMPROVEMENT OF THE GRASSHOPPER STUDY

The reader may recall that one of the main purposes of a theory is to suggest new ways of conceptualizing old observations and previous research findings. In Chapter 3, an experiment was presented which tested the effect of communicator credibility on attitude change. It was assumed (and found) that the more credible a communicator, the more attitude change a standard communication should produce. However, dissonance theory suggests one condition under which high credibility may lead to less attitude change than low credibility. Such a condition occurs if the person is induced to engage in *counterattitudinal behavior.*

This prediction depends on two important points. First of all, it is assumed that the credibility of a communicator can be separated into two sets of traits. One set refers to aspects of the communicator which are relevant to the particular communication being presented. Examples of such traits are the amount of knowledge the communicator has about the topic (expertise), and the gains he can make by getting his audience to change their attitudes (trustworthiness). The second set of traits refers to aspects which are irrelevant to the communication (for example, whether the communicator is male or female, whether or not he is a nice guy, etc.).

The second important point is that in order for dissonance to be produced in the first place, the subject must engage in overt *counterattitudinal behavior* rather than just hear a communication. Dissonance theory suggests that if a person is forced to engage in discrepant behavior by a communicator who has a lot of irrelevant *negative* traits, there will be more dissonance than if he is induced to do so by a communicator who has a lot of irrelevant *positive* traits. This derivation is based on the assumption that the irrelevant positive traits are cognitive elements consonant with engaging in the act requested by the communicator ("I did it because he's a nice guy."). The negative irrelevant traits, however, cannot serve as justification for complying. Engaging in the act at the request of a negative communicator should, therefore, create greater dissonance.

A forced-compliance experiment which was conducted by Zimbardo, Weisenberg, Firestone, and Levy (1965) was derived from the above theory. One reason for conducting this particular experiment, aside from its practical implications and nonintuitive predictions, was that it corrected procedural faults found in the Smith study (1961), which claimed to test the same hypotheses (and which was critically reviewed in the previous chapter). For a theory to be adequately tested, the hypotheses derived from the theory must be tested by experiments which are procedurally well executed.

The basic *conceptual* hypotheses derived from dissonance theory were: If a subject complies with the request of a communicator who has negative, communication-irrelevant traits, he will experience more dissonance than if he complies with a communicator who has positive, communication-irrelevant traits. If the cognition about the behavioral commitment is more resistant to change than cognitions about one's attitude toward the behavior, then attitude change will be the major dissonance reducing mechanism. The prediction, then, is that more attitude change should occur following compliance with the negative than with the positive communicator. Note that this prediction is opposite to the intuitive notion we considered before, namely that a positive (high credibility) communicator should produce more change than a negative (low credibility) communicator. Let us see how these conceptual hypotheses were translated into operations.

Attitudes toward eating a highly disliked food—fried grasshoppers—were measured before and immediately after an inducement to eat the food was made by a communicator who adopted a friendly, positive role for half the subjects and an unfriendly, negative role for the others.

Communicator Characteristics

Because the communicator in both experimental roles was an officer in the college's ROTC program, it was possible to determine how he was usually perceived by means of responses on an alleged officer-rating survey. From the personality trait profile which emerged from this analysis, a set of experimental role behaviors was developed. In addition, *both* the positive and the negative communicator had to be perceived as possessing a number of positive traits necessary for effective execution of the experiment. Thus the communicator had to be seen by all subjects as conscientious, capable, well organized, concerned about the reactions of the subjects, and industrious.

Positive role. The communicator (playing the role of an experimenter) interacted with his "assistant" according to a prearranged script in which, for the positive condition, he gave politely phrased requests to the assistant, called him by his first name, responded to a "mistake" by the assistant with equanimity, and in general was considerate and pleasant. But at all times it was clear that he was the person in charge of the experiment and in control.

Negative role. However, the negative condition demanded that the communicator be perceived as unpleasant, a person one would not want to know, work with, or work for. This perception of the negative communicator was largely induced by his quite formal interaction with the assistant. When the assistant mistakenly brought in the "wrong" experimental food (a tray of eels in aspic instead of grasshoppers), the communicator, who was in the process of talking to the subjects in his most pleasant manner, suddenly blew up and said, "Oh, dammit, can't you remember the schedule? That food is for the next group. . . . Let's get with it and hurry up about it!" As the assistant left, obviously embarrassed, the communicator shrugged his shoulders disgustedly, then *reversed his role behavior in front of the subjects* and proceeded again in the same tone as previously.

The reader should compare these positive and negative roles with those used in the Smith study. The effect of these role variations, as well as the validity of the measuring instruments, was first tested in a laboratory setting with the college subjects; the roles were then slightly modified to make them appropriate for army reservists.

Procedure

The subjects first completed a nine-point attitude scale of degree of liking for a wide range of food items, including the fried Japanese grasshopper. Following the initial attitude measurements, the subjects were assigned to the various conditions in the experiment. Differences in the communicator's role behavior commenced as soon as the subjects entered the experimental room. After they completed a hunger and eating habit questionnaire, heard a talk about the needs of the new mobile army, and witnessed the assistant's "mistake," a plate with five fried grasshoppers was placed in front of each of the men. The experimenter tried to induce the subjects to eat a grasshopper, although maintaining that their action was completely voluntary. Every subject had to make some overt response whether they chose to eat or not, but that response could only be seen by the experimenter.

Control groups were also used, in which subjects were not given an inducement or opportunity to eat a grasshopper but their attitudes were measured before and after a time interval equivalent to that of the experimental groups.

Post-Compliance Attitudes

The final ratings, which were made in a third room, were in the *absence* of the "experimenter-communicator." The assistant of the alleged civilian liaison told the subjects that he wanted to evaluate various aspects of the experiment and get more information from them. At this time the experimental subjects completed:

1. a post-measure of attitudes toward a number of foods, including grasshoppers;

2. a measure of willingness to endorse eating grasshoppers (a second measure of attitude, more linked to action);

3. checks on the experimental conditions of choice, pressure, etc. (assessing some of the general experimental conditions);

4. several indexes of evaluation of both the communicator and his assistant (assessing the independent variable).

Results

The main results of the study are the attitude change scores from the pre- to post-measures of liking for fried grasshoppers. However, other information is also important. For example, in all groups about fifty percent of the men ate (the mean being two grasshoppers). Thus there was no initial difference in overt behavioral compliance. Also, results from a rating scale indicated that the subjects felt they had complete freedom of choice in eating the grasshoppers. Furthermore, it appears that the manipulated differences in the communicator traits were perceived by the subjects exactly as intended.

The attitude change results were presented in terms of the net percent of subjects who increased their liking for the grasshoppers. If the dissonance theory prediction is correct, the subjects who ate the grasshoppers for the negative communicator should have increased their liking more than those who ate the grasshopper for the positive communicator. This was exactly the result, with the absolute effect being quite large—fifty percent more change in the negative than in the positive communicator treatment. This result was, of course, statistically significant. The control groups (without the discrepant commitment) showed practically no net change in attitudes.

This result replicates, with the proper controls and a somewhat improved procedure, the earlier findings we questioned in Chapter 4. Such *systematic replication* is one crucial test of a theory. The dissonance findings hold when different subject populations (college students and army reservists) and different experimental conditions are utilized. Furthermore, the magnitude of the attitude change produced by the manipulations is much greater than that found in the credibility studies, which tested the intuitive credibility hypothesis in a situation that permitted "free-listening exposure."

EXTENSION OF THE MINIMAL JUSTIFICATION EFFECT

This replication of the finding that a negative communicator can be an effective agent of attitude change provides considerable support for the hypotheses relating attitude change to justification for a discrepant commitment. However, the power of the theory could be more convincingly demonstrated if the same hypothesis were tested using completely different operations of each of the conceptual variables (of justification, discrepant behavioral commitment, dissonance reduction, and attitude). Festinger and Carlsmith (1959) did just this in what has become a classic study in social psychology.

College students were asked to perform a boring task as part of a psychology experiment. The task consisted of rotating blocks, which were mounted on pegs, for one full hour. The task seemed to have no specific purpose. After the task was completed, subjects were randomly placed into one of three groups: high, low, or no dissonance. In the high and low dissonance groups the experimenter asked the subject to help him out. He explained that his regular assistant could not make it that day and asked the subject to take his place. He then said that the main purpose of the study, which the subject had presumably just completed, was to see the effect on performance (of the peg-turning task) of different "sets" about the task. The subject was told that he was in the group in which subjects were not informed about the nature of the task. Other subjects were allegedly told that the task was enjoyable. This job was usually performed by the regular assistant.

Another subject (really a confederate) was coming any minute. The experimenter asked the real subject to lie to the new arrival, saying that the boring task which he had just completed was really enjoyable. For doing this, the experimenter offered twenty dollars in the low dissonance group, or one dollar in the high dissonance group. The control group was not asked to lie about the task, but merely waited alone for four minutes. These procedures not only varied the incentives for lying, but allowed standardized feedback from the person to whom the subject thought he was lying.

After the four-minute sessions with the confederates (or the four-minute wait) all groups went to an interviewer whom they had not seen before (an attempt to separate the response measure from the experiment proper). He had the subject fill out four rating scales on various aspects of the experiment.

The only statistically significant results were found on the scale asking the subjects how enjoyable the tasks were. The condition in which subjects were asked to lie and were given only one dollar had a more positive mean rating than either the twenty dollar condition or the control condition. In other words, when subjects were asked to lie about a boring job for a minimal amount of justification (one dollar), they experienced dissonance. This dissonance was reduced by the subjects' changing one of the dissonant elements in a more consonant direction; namely, they claimed that they liked the task more.

Unfortunately, this experiment has a number of flaws. The most glaring one deals with the justification manipulation. Twenty dollars may not be on the same scale as one dollar. Twenty dollars may arouse suspicion or guilt on the part of the subjects taking the money. What psychology experiment ever offered anyone twenty dollars? In addition, about fourteen percent of the subjects had to be excluded from the final data analysis, some for suspicion and others for refusing to accept the money.

To correct these flaws, a *parametric* study was conducted by Cohen (1962). Instead of being induced to say that a boring task was enjoyable, subjects were induced to write an essay against their own attitude position. Subjects were then given either fifty cents, one dollar, five dollars, or ten dollars as justification for the discrepant behavior. If dissonance theory is correct, there should be maximum dissonance in the fifty cents condition, and therefore most attitude change toward the essay (assuming that attitude change is the main method of dissonance reduction). Cohen did find a linear effect: most attitude change in the fifty cents condition, and least in the ten dollar condition. In conclusion, a test of the *same* conceptual hypothesis as that in the grasshopper studies, by experiments using very different specific operations for both the independent and dependent variables, turned out to support the hypothesis derived from dissonance theory.

INITIATION RITES AND ATTITUDE CHANGE

While systematic replication of *one* hypothesis derived from a theory supports the use of the conceptual variables in that hypothesis (in the experiments which have been presented so far, they were justification, attitude-discrepant behavior, and attitude change), it does not provide great support for *other* concepts in the theory. In order for the theory itself to be supported, hypotheses which use different conceptual variables, as well as different operations, must be derived from the theory. These hypotheses must then be supported by research designed to test them.

The derivation of these hypotheses should be based on the rules given by the theory for manipulating the symbols (concepts) of the theory. These rules, in the theory of cognitive dissonance, are essentially grammatical and semantic. That is, a researcher derives hypotheses from the theory on the basis of how the concepts are grammatically related to each other. The statement, "If magnitude of dissonance increases, then the need for dissonance reduction increases," is a logical-grammatical rule relating the two conceptual variables, "magnitude of dissonance" and "dissonance reduction." Let us see how another hypothesis was derived from dissonance theory and how it was tested experimentally.

The grasshopper and boring-task studies had theoretical importance, in that they were designed to test a nonobvious prediction about the effect of justification on attitude change. However, they did not have much direct practical relevance. It is rare that you would want to change someone's liking of a food such as grasshoppers, or of an activity like peg-turning. However, a problem which seems very relevant to most college students is how people become attracted to groups, such as fraternities or militant organizations. Very often these groups require a great amount of work from individual members or applicants, while they provide little real gratification in return. For example, fraternities often demand that their pledges go through embarrassing, often painful, and very inconvenient activities which are irrelevant to the functioning of the fraternity (or to reasons for wanting to belong to it). Intuitively, it would seem that these initiations would produce dislike of the group on the part of the pledges. However, cognitive dissonance theory has something different to say about this situation.

The knowledge that a person has experienced a painful and embarrassing initiation is, in effect, a cognition. Furthermore, the knowledge that the group or organization into which the person had to be initiated was unattractive would be a cognition dissonant with the previous one. If the group is unattractive, a person feels he should not have to undergo a painful and embarrassing initiation. As the initiation becomes more and more painful, the magnitude of dissonance should increase. How can dissonance be reduced? Since the person has been committed to the painfulness of the initiation (that is, he has publicly behaved in ways leading to embarrassment), it is most likely that dissonance will be reduced by the person's *increasing* his liking for the group. By increasing his liking, he can better justify his having experienced a painful initiation. Using the previously mentioned "magnitude of dissonance" rule, we should predict that as the initiation becomes more severe (or as the magnitude of initial dissonance increases), the attraction to the group should increase (or the amount of dissonance reduction should increase). A study by Aronson and Mills (1959) was designed especially to test this derivation from dissonance theory.

Female subjects volunteered to participate in a group discussion on the psychology of sex. Three conditions were run in the study: severe initiation (high dissonance), mild initiation (low dissonance), and a control group. In the severe initiation condition, the subjects were required to read aloud a list of twelve obscene words and two vivid descriptions of sexual activity. In the mild initiation condition, they were required to read five words which were related to sex but not obscene. The control group was not required to read aloud.

After having read the materials, the subjects were told that they had performed satisfactorily and could join a meeting that was then in progress. The experimenter suggested that since the subject was not prepared for that particular meeting, she should merely listen over earphones and not participate in the group discussion. In this way, she could get some idea of how the group discussions operated. Unknown to the subjects, a tape recorder presented a prerecorded tape of a *standardized* discussion. The discussion was devised by the experimenters to appear very boring. The participants spoke dryly, hemmed, hawed, and contradicted themselves. After the discussion was completed, the subject was told that each participant always filled out scales rating both the discussion and the participants. These ratings were the dependent variables of "attitudes toward the group."

The results suggested that female subjects who read the obscene words liked both the group activity and the group members more than either females who read nonobscene words or the controls who did not read anything.

At first glance, a new hypothesis derived directly from dissonance theory seems to have been supported. As the theory suggested, the more severe an initiation, the greater the dissonance (and the dissonance reduction) produced when the group turns out to be unsatisfying.

Unfortunately, as the reader may have noted, there are a number of alternative ways of conceptualizing these results. The subjects in the severe initiation condition passed a more difficult test to get into the group, and therefore, they may have been more satisfied with their performance. Or, the high sexual content of the severe initiation may have suggested that future group discussions would be more interesting, even though the present one was not up to the subject's expectations. Thus, two major problems with this experiment seem to involve the feedback to the subjects that they passed the test and the close relationship between the nature of the initiation and the content of the group activity.

It may be recalled that the content of real life initiation rites is often irrelevant (pain, embarrassment) to the group's primary purposes and functions. Such activities are designed to be hurdles or means of ensuring exclusivity, rather than tests of adequacy. A study by Gerard and Mathewson (1966) corrected these problems by using physical pain (electric shocks) as the initiation and by controlling for the test feedback. The results of their systematic replication still supported dissonance theory. The more severe the initiation (the more the pain), the more the subjects liked a boring group discussion, whether or not they were told they had passed the pain test! Thus, the support for dissonance theory mounts.

EXTENSION OF THE CONCEPT OF DISSONANCE REDUCTION

The reader should have noted that although the operations for producing dissonance have varied in these different experiments, the measure of dissonance reduction (attitude change) has always been self-ratings on scales dealing with how much something (an object, a task, or a group) was liked. Dissonance theory should also be able to predict differences in other operational measures of dissonance reduction. If the concept of "dissonance reduction" is to have any utility, it should be demonstrated that by using the concept and correspondence rules of the theory new measurement operations can be derived. These new measures should show the same effect as the other operations of dissonance reduction when tested in a new experiment derived from the theory. A study by Cohen, Greenbaum, and Mansson (1963) was designed to test such an extension of dissonance theory. The experiment studied the rate of verbal use of personal pronouns, i.e., I and we. Social reinforcement was effective in increasing their use when subjects voluntarily committed themselves for *high* justification to a period of social approval deprivation. However, social reinforcement was ineffective when minimal justification was given.

By predicting a change in the rate at which personal pronouns are emitted, dissonance theory has been extended to new behavior and thus its generality has been increased. The rate of emission of personal pronouns may, in fact, be a crucial determiner of one's own attitude towards oneself. Saying "I" more and more might make the person seem more self-centered to others. Perhaps even the subject's perception of himself is guided by similar observations of his own behavior (see Bem, 1967).

Although this is obviously a limited survey of the evidence for the theory, it should be sufficient to provide a feel for how the theory functions. We should now be in a position to critically evaluate the theory as a prelude to determining how it can help generate techniques applicable to the solution of practical problems.

CRITICAL ANALYSIS OF DISSONANCE THEORY

In the same way that it was possible to generate new and interesting techniques of change by critically evaluating single experiments, it should also be possible to generate new ideas for producing change by critically evaluating a theory, provided that a creative attitude is maintained during the process. In order to evaluate the utility of one theory in comparison to another (or to *no* theory), we first have to know what is meant by the utility of a theory. Typically, the utility of a theory is judged on the basis of (1) the new research to which it leads, (2) the generality of the theory (or the number of seemingly different phenomena or results which it explains), (3) the degree to which the theory adequately explains and predicts the results which it was intended to predict, and (4) its parsimony (or its lack of unnecessary and superfluous concepts). In addition, a theory is often evaluated by the degree to which it can be expanded or internally changed to explain findings and phenomena which were not accounted for by the original theory. To what extent does dissonance theory meet these criteria?

First of all, one point in favor of dissonance theory is that it has stimulated a great deal of interesting research in social psychology. Most of it would not have been conducted had it not been for dissonance theory. Over and above the theory's ability to stimulate new research, to what extent can it "adequately" explain and predict the results which experimenters claim were derived from the theory? In order to answer this question, the reader should be asking himself other questions about the theory. How might a theory be inadequate? Are its correspondence rules clearly stated? What about the rules which relate the various concepts to one another? Are they outlined, and if so, how specific are they? How does dissonance theory stand up to these questions?

At the beginning of the section on dissonance theory it was stated that the central concept was "inconsistency", or "dissonance" between cognitive elements. However, since dissonance theory makes predictions based on the "magnitude of dissonance," rather than merely the presence or absence of "dissonance," we can consider the central concept of the theory to be the "magnitude of dissonance." What is the status of this concept in the theory? Is it an operation, a conceptual variable, or a hypothetical construct? As the theory now stands, this concept is a hypothetical construct. As such, it is not directly related to operations but, instead, is related to other concepts in the theory which, in turn, are related to operations. In fact, the hypothetical construct "magnitude of dissonance" is related to two sets of concepts. One set is the independent variables and the other is the dependent variables in the theory. Therefore, we can ask what rules relate the central construct to the independent variables and, furthermore, what rules relate it to the dependent variables.

Taking the independent variables first, the concepts which are directly related to the "magnitude of dissonance" are: (1) the ratio of dissonant to consonant elements, (2) the importance of the elements, and (3) the cognitive overlap between these elements. What is the nature of the rules which link these concepts to the concept of "magnitude of dissonance?" Essentially, they are grammatical or semi-logical rules. Specifically, the *greater* the "ratio of dissonant to consonant elements," the *greater* the "magnitude of dissonance." The *more* "important" the elements, the *greater* the "magnitude of dissonance," etc. The rule which is abstracted from these examples is, "the more of *X*, the greater the *Y*." One then asks how much more of *X* is required to produce greater *Y*. In the "ratio of dissonant to consonant elements" rule, how much greater ratio is really greater? The rule leaves ambiguous the exact mathematical relation of *X* to *Y*. Instead, the rule relies on the experimenter's intuition of what "more" and "greater" mean, and relates *X* and *Y* by a verbal statement whose meaning depends upon its grammatical structure. Since one man's grammatical structure is another man's nonsense, we are again faced with ambiguity and the necessity for the experimenter to use his intuition in discovering the meaning of these rules.

Even though the rules which relate the conceptual independent variables to the main hypothetical construct are ambiguous, we can still ask what the correspondence rules are which relate the conceptual independent variables to specific operations or manipulations of events in the world.

How do we arrange our experimental procedures to produce varying ratios of dissonant to consonant cognitive elements? How do we derive specific operations to vary "importance?" It is here that dissonance theory can be most severely criticized. The theory merely states that *any* operations which produce two cognitive elements such that one of the cognitive elements follows from the psychologically obverse of the other will produce two "dissonant elements." The theory leaves "psychologically obverse" and "cognitive element" undefined, again relying on the intuition of the experimenter. What is a cognitive element? How do we manipulate beliefs, opinions, or bits of knowledge? How many events in the world equal one cognitive element? All of these questions are unanswered by the theory. The concepts of "justification" and "commitment" are in a similarly undefined state in the theory. For example, is more justification produced by giving a subject three reasons why he should perform a behavior discrepant with his attitudes, or is more produced by giving him two dollars? Furthermore, is a subject more (or less) committed to a discrepant behavior if he is asked to give a counterattitudinal speech on a tape which will then be played to a thousand people, or if he is asked to give the same speech live to a group of twenty people?

What about the conceptual dependent variables? The main conceptual dependent variable in dissonance theory is "need for dissonance reduction." The hypothetical construct "magnitude of dissonance" is linked to this dependent concept, as it was to the independent concepts, by a grammatical rule. That is, the *greater* the "magnitude of dissonance" the *greater* the "need to reduce dissonance." This rule faces the same ambiguities (and more) as those for the conceptual independent variables. Since the concept "need for dissonance reduction" is itself linked to other concepts rather than to operations, we can consider "need for dissonance reduction" another hypothetical construct. Thus both the construct "magnitude of dissonance" and the construct "need for dissonance reduction" are hypothetical, with the first being directly related to conceptual independent variables, and the second being directly related to conceptual dependent variables. These latter variables are: (1) revoking a decision, (2) lowering the importance of the cognitive elements, (3) increasing the cognitive overlap between cognitive elements, (4) adding consonant elements, (5) eliminating dissonant elements, and (6) making relevant elements irrelevant. As before, the rules relating "need for dissonance reduction" to these conceptual dependent variables are grammatical ones, of the "if more of *X,* then more of *Y*" variety.

However, there is additional ambiguity, over and above that built into this kind of rule. No mention is made in the theory of *which* of these many modes of "dissonance reduction" will be employed in a given situation. Furthermore, no mention is made of how reduction of dissonance by one means affects the reduction we can expect by another means. To put it another way, we do not know how these many methods of dissonance reduction interact with each other.

How does the theory get us back to the real world, to the behavior of subjects? What are the correspondence rules linking these dependent concepts to behavior? Unfortunately, as with the operations for the conceptual independent variables, there are none. However, the following are just some of the ways which Festinger offers as means for reducing dissonance: the subject can change toward the advocated position; he can try to influence the communicator to change; he can seek social support to maintain his original position or to bolster his changed position; he can derogate the communicator; he can deny the link between the communicator and the communication; he can distort its content or fail to perceive its implications. By specifying so many operational techniques for reducing dissonance, the theory increases the number of phenomena to which it can apply (which is to its advantage). However, because the theory does not tell us exactly how to relate these operations to the many conceptually distinct modes of dissonance reduction, and because it does not tell us how these methods of reduction interact, the theory can predict almost *any* result which an experiment might find.

For example, if in the grasshopper studies subjects who ate grasshoppers for the negative communicator did *not* change their liking for the grasshoppers, the theory could "explain" such a result by claiming that dissonance was instead reduced by the subject perceiving the originally negative communicator as more positive (if such a result occurred). What should normally be a *disconfirmation* of a hypothesis derived from dissonance theory can instead be changed into support for the theory. Such a situation means that we are never sure *before* an experiment is conducted which of the many possible results will occur.

Because dissonance theory was not stated as clearly as it might have been, experimenters conducting research designed to test predictions derived from the theory have often incorrectly translated the theory into specific operations. For example, we have seen how the "magnitude of justification" has been one crucial conceptual independent variable in many experiments. The theory states that the magnitude of justification varies as a direct function (what kind of function is not stated) of the *number* or *importance* of the consonant elements. For example, as the number of positive traits of a communicator increases, justification for complying increases. However, in many experiments, rather than manipulating the number (or the importance) of the consonant (justification) elements, a single element was varied. As an example, the Festinger and Carlsmith study used *amount* of money to vary justification for engaging in a discrepant behavior. That is, some subjects received one dollar and other subjects received twenty dollars. Does twenty dollars (the high justification element) differ from one dollar in the *number* or in the *importance* of the elements consonant with complying? The answer is unclear. Furthermore, the results from all experiments which have used money as a justification yielded contradictions: some studies showed more attitude change with less monetary incentive, while others showed the opposite or no effect.

Such inconsistency is not unexpected, even if we accept the theory. These "manipulations of justification" have not been properly linked to the concept of "justification" as the theory defines it. In other words, experimenters have not adequately "fit" the concepts in the theory to events in the world. Therefore, if the results from these experiments appear not to support the theory, it could be because these experiments are not *adequate tests* of the theory, or because the theory does not apply to these particular experiments.

By approaching the theory critically, we may be able to determine which experiments are adequate tests of the theory and which are not. Unfortunately, the theory itself does not tell us what operations stated here are adequate. There are no rules which relate number or importance of cognitive elements to specific manipulations of events in the world (like money, number of verbally stated reasons, etc.). This deficiency may explain why experiments which *do* seem, on intuitive grounds, to fit the theory have found results inconsistent with the theory's predictions. A theory which can not predict results, either because it is wrong, or because it is ambiguously stated, is a relatively useless theory.

On the other hand, although dissonance theory does contain a number of flaws in structure, the reader should not forget that the theory has suggested many new and interesting techniques for attitude and behavior change.

In Chapter 6, we shall see how a specific practical problem was solved using some techniques derived directly from dissonance theory.

Furthermore, dissonance theory has made clear a conceptual relationship between behavior and attitude change that has never been explicitly stated before. It attempts to specify the conditions under which changes in behavior will be followed by corresponding changes in attitudes. Previously, the relationship was seen only in the opposite direction—that is, how changes in attitudes affected behavior. In effect, dissonance theory has suggested a new technique which can be used to produce attitude change. This technique (inducing people to engage in counterattitudinal behavior for a minimal number of reasons, especially when they feel they have free choice) can be used to solve a number of the practical problems presented throughout this book. Furthermore, by critically evaluating the theory, we have been able to determine which methods for producing justification should be more (or less) effective when trying to apply this technique.

In summary, it appears that dissonance theory (as with most things in life) has both good and bad points. It has generated much interesting and creative research in social psychology. It has supplied us with some new techniques for producing attitude change. It has related many phenomena which were previously thought to be unrelated. On the other hand, the theory has not *adequately* explained or predicted its results. Furthermore, the theory lacks a clearly stated internal structure which can be related to external events in some obvious manner. All in all, the theory has been useful, but unless it is overhauled, its future utility will be unrealized.

BEHAVIOR OR ATTITUDE CHANGE?

One of the most useful ideas which our critical analysis of dissonance theory has generated is the relationship between attitudes and behavior change. Up to now, we have implicitly assumed that attitudes are generalized predispositions to behave in various ways (see Chapter 1). It follows from this conception that changes in these predispositions should be followed by corresponding changes in behavior. Furthermore, such changes in attitudes should produce *enduring and general* changes in behavior if attitudes are themselves enduring and generalized. Research relevant to this topic has unfortunately indicated that such a conclusion is false (Mischel, 1968). Changes in attitude are not necessarily accompanied by changes in behavior. Furthermore, when changes in behavior do occur, they are rarely, if ever, general or enduring.

It seems that we are faced with a real problem. Most practical situations in which we wish to induce change require that *both* attitude and behavior change be produced. If, however, behavior change does not automatically follow from attitude change, how can attitude change techniques help us solve the practical problems? Can dissonance theory help? Unfortunately, it cannot. The theory does suggest methods which will produce attitude change following behavior change, but it does not suggest how to produce or maintain the changes in behavior. All is not lost. Another approach (called social learning) does suggest techniques for producing and maintaining behavior change and for producing change in what we have been conceptualizing as attitudes. This approach (which weds learning theory and social psychology) could also be used to solve the problem with which this chapter began, namely inconsistency in the methodology and results in attitude change research.

SOCIAL LEARNING APPROACH

Rather than defining the social learning approach abstractly, as we defined dissonance theory, we will explain it by setting forth the techniques it uses.

RESPONSE-REINFORCEMENT RELATIONSHIPS

The social learning approach conceives of most human behavior as leading to consequences which *feed back* to the behavior, either maintaining or changing the probability of similar behavior in the future. For example, when a child touches a stove (behavior) and then gets burned (consequence), it is likely that he will not touch the same stove in the future. If another child's touching the stove had been followed by a different consequence (his mother gave him some candy), then the likelihood that he would perform similar acts in the future would be different from that of the child who was burned. Furthermore, it is assumed that the mechanism by which the child's future behavior is changed is a form of learning. The basic idea here is that the likelihood of a specific response is determined by the consequences which the person expects will follow the performance of that response. If the consequences are positive or rewarding, the behavior is likely to recur. If they are negative or punishing (fear-arousing, etc.), the behavior is not likely to recur.

LEARNING RESPONSE-REINFORCEMENT RELATIONS

Learning can proceed by any number of techniques. A person can directly experience the consequence of his own behavior. When a black child asks a teacher about black history and the teacher ignores the child, the child will learn that if he wishes to find out about black history, asking his teacher (response) will not lead to answers (consequences).

People can also learn by looking. That is, they can see how other people's behavior is followed by specific consequences. Another black child in the same class will learn, merely by watching how the other child's questions go unanswered, not to ask questions about black history. This technique of learning by observation has also been called "modeling," "observational learning," and "vicarious learning."

People can also learn by listening or reading. That is, they can learn by acting like theorists. They hear people talk about how specific behaviors and consequences are related. That is, they hear that if X is done, then Y will occur. From these symbolic rules they can learn that the behavior which X represents will probably be followed by the consequences which Y represents. For example, one can easily learn by reading newspaper reports that if one were to call a policeman a "pig" during a riot, a bash over the head would be likely to follow.

LEARNING STIMULUS-STIMULUS RELATIONS

Other kinds of "if-then" relationships can also be learned. For example, one can learn which emotional states (sexual arousal, fear, etc.) are likely to be produced by various stimuli. Such learning can proceed by direct experience, by observing others, or by hearing or reading about symbolic relationships between stimuli and emotional responses. For example, people can be emotionally aroused, either negatively or positively, by certain words such as "Jew," "cop," "commie," without having *directly* experienced negative or positive consequences when faced with the real people represented by these words. Thus, the word "Negro" can arouse a negative emotional state in some people simply because the word has been associated with other words which produce negative arousal, such as "bad," "dirty," "stupid," "lustful," etc. In more general terms, people can learn that certain stimuli are associated with other stimuli. By learning these stimulus-stimulus relationships, previously neutral stimuli can come to arouse negative or positive emotions, or stimuli which were previously arousing can come to be neutral. Thus it is possible for some people to be emotionally aroused by what seem (to other people) to be neutral stimuli simply because they have learned a different set of associations for such stimuli.

DISCRIMINATION AND GENERALIZATION

When people learn "if-then" relationships, they typically do not learn them in a vacuum. They also learn the conditions under which these relationships are true. For example, a child eventually learns that only when a stove is on (or has just been turned off) is he likely to be burned if he touches it. When the stove has been off for a long time, touching it will lead to a different set of consequences (not being burned). In this way, people *discriminate* between situations or stimulus events. They learn to expect *different* consequences for the same behavior when different stimulus conditions are present.

On the other hand, people can also generalize situations to some extent. One may feel that almost all "cops" (rather than just one) are likely to club people who call them "pigs." When variations in stimulus situations are responded to in similar ways, the person is said to *generalize* across these situations. When he responds differently to variations, it is said that he *discriminates*. For example, seeing a murderer in jail will elicit much less emotional arousal than seeing the same murderer in a dark alley.

THE "STUFF" OF LEARNING

The social learning approach essentially assumes that the "stuff" of learning is bits of information, such as, if X then Y, or X goes with Y, or Z occurs only when X and Y do, etc. These specific bits of information are assumed to be stored in the organism. How these bits of information will affect behavior is a function of the X's, Y's and Z's in the relationships. For example, we would expect behavior to be very different if the Z were reward instead of punishment. Whether or not a particular bit of information will affect behavior is a function of the stimulus conditions or situations in which a person finds himself at any given moment. Thus the "stuff" of learning is a set of relationships between both behavioral and stimulus events.

SOME SPECIFIC TECHNIQUES FOR CHANGING THE "STUFF"

Direct reinforcement is one technique for changing behavior. The basic idea is that a person will learn if we change the consequences of his behavior and have him directly experience them. To get a person to perform a complex behavior, this technique often requires that we "shape" him by having him perform a graded sequence of steps of increasing difficulty. For example, we may want someone to shoot a gun accurately. In order to get him to do this, we first have to make the consequences of merely holding a gun *explicit* and *positive.* That is, the person must learn that he can avoid punishment or gain reward by holding the gun in a certain way. Once he has learned how to do this, we can make avoiding punishment not only contingent on holding the gun, but also on aiming it, holding it steady, squeezing the trigger, etc. In this way, a person comes to learn new responses and to experience directly the consequences of these responses.

Extinction is another technique for manipulating behavior. In order to get a person to stop a particular behavior, we merely prevent the consequences which he expects will follow his action from occurring, while letting him continue to perform the behavior. For example, if someone dominates a group discussion because he likes to argue, one way to reduce the amount of time he talks would be to remove the consequences maintaining his dominating behavior, namely, get everyone to ignore him when he talked.

Vicarious reinforcement and vicarious extinction are often useful techniques. The results obtained by using direct experience can sometimes be obtained more efficiently by having the person see other people performing in a certain way and receiving rewards or punishments as a result. If a person were afraid to talk in public because he felt people were critical of public speakers, then one way to increase the likelihood of his public speaking would be to show him a number of people speaking in public and being praised rather than criticized.

Instructions, rules, or communications can all be used to change behavior. The technique is to present the person with rules (or symbolic, verbally stated, response-reinforcement relationships) which are different from those which the person believes are true. For example, a prejudiced person might expect that if he were to get close to a Negro, he would find that the Negro was dirty. One way to change this expectancy would be to present this person with statements about (1) how Negroes are not dirty, (2) how other people do not think Negroes are dirty, etc. (in effect, present him with a persuasive communication).

A related technique is to train people to present *themselves* with their own instructions, rules, and symbolic reinforcements or punishments. That is, people are trained to give themselves persuasive messages in particular circumstances. For example, we might want to train a policeman to say to himself: "This person is a nice, wonderful human being who deserves only the best from me." The conditions under which we might train him to say this would be whenever he was called a "pig" by someone during a riot.

TWO EXAMPLES OF THE SOCIAL LEARNING APPROACH

Let us look at two experiments derived from the social learning approach which deal with verbal, nonverbal, and emotional responses. The first experiment was conducted by Gordon Paul (1966) and the second by Bandura, Blanchard, and Ritter (1968). Both of these experiments involve a technique called desensitization. Essentially, it is a learning technique in which subjects learn a new set of *emotional* responses to an old stimulus. For example, a fear-arousing stimulus can become a neutral or positive stimulus, or vice versa. In the case of fear, a subject is first taught how to relax completely (a response which is incompatible with fear). After this training, symbolic representations of the fear-arousing situation are presented in a graded hierarchical form, from very nonarousing to very arousing, *while the subject remains deeply relaxed.* In this way, once the training is complete, the fear-arousing stimulus comes to elicit relaxation rather than fear responses.

In the first study, subjects volunteered to participate in the experiment because they were afraid of speaking in public. These subjects were randomly assigned to one of four conditions: desensitization, insight (traditional clinical therapy), an attention-placebo control, and a nontreatment control group. The insight condition consisted of various forms of the traditional long-term client-therapist interview. At the close of the interview, the therapist provided the client with an insight into the nature and cause of his speech phobia. The subjects in the attention-placebo control group were provided with useless placebos (said to reduce tension and anxiety) along with warm and understanding attention centering around the subject's "problem." The final control group received only a pre-post measure of the dependent variables. There were three before-after treatment measurements on all subjects: (1) ratings by unbiased observers of the subject's ability to actually give speeches in public, (2) self-report measures of anxiety during speeches, (3) physiological measures of arousal (heart rate, etc.).

The results can be stated quite simply. The desensitization, insight, and attention-placebo conditions produced highly significant reductions in self-reported anxiety which were greater than those for the nontreatment control group. On the other hand, only the desensitization group almost completely eliminated the overt fear of speaking in public. Only in this group were almost all of the subjects able to speak in public without overt signs of fear or physiologically measured affective arousal. Stated another way, verbal self-ratings of fear (attitudes toward public speaking) were changed equally well by each of the three treatments. However, actual public speaking behavior and the physiological measures of fear were affected only by the treatment derived from the social learning approach (desensitization).

Why should such a result be found? What makes verbal self-ratings equally sensitive to each treatment, while the nonverbal measures are affected only by one? The answer lies in the nature of the treatments. Each of them includes a large degree of verbal activity on the part of the subjects and experimenter. In the attention-placebo treatment, subjects are essentially *told* not to be fearful and given placebos which are supposed to make them less fearful. In the insight therapy treatment, the subjects are again *told* not to be fearful, and are also supplied with reinforcement from the therapist whenever they label themselves as less fearful. Thus in both these treatments, subjects are given reinforcement and attention for *talking* about themselves as being less fearful. On the other hand, subjects do not learn how to be less fearful (to relax) in these two treatments. In the desensitization treatment, however, subjects *do* learn how to be less fearful when faced with symbolic fear stimuli (usually verbal descriptions of public speaking). Once they learn not to be afraid, they correctly label themselves as less fearful.[1] Subjects receiving the other two treatments learn only how to *rate* themselves as less fearful, but not how to *be* less fearful in public speaking situations. From this study we can see how one class of behavior (attitudes, or self-ratings) can be controlled by one general set of stimuli, while another related class of behavior can be controlled by a different set of stimuli (the desensitization procedure).

The second study compared the desensitization technique with live modeling and with a no-treatment control (and with other conditioning

---

[1] It should be noted that by labeling themselves as less fearful *after* giving a speech in public, the subjects are behaving in a manner predicted by dissonance theory. That is, they are bringing their attitudes (self-descriptions) in line with their behavior.

techniques). The purpose of this study was to determine which treatment method would produce the most behavioral change, and which treatments would also change self-ratings. Subjects were initially selected because they were highly fearful of snakes. The live modeling group saw a model handle a snake without showing any signs of fear while doing so. The desensitization group associated verbally presented snake stimuli with relaxation. The results demonstrated that live models produced a greater increase in *overt* handling of snakes than either the desensitization group or no-treatment control group. On the other hand, verbally stated attitudes were affected by both treatments.

Why should both of these treatments affect self-ratings, but only one treatment affect overt behavior? As in the previous study, the answer lies in the specific details of each treatment. In the live modeling treatments, subjects learn that "*if* people touch snakes, *then* nothing bad happens to them." That is, they learn that punishments are not likely to follow the handling of most snakes. However, in the desensitization treatment, subjects learn to relax while thinking about or hearing about snakes, and they do not *necessarily* learn that touching snakes will not lead to punishment. That is, they learn to relax when they hear, read, or think about snakes but not when they actually have to touch one. Thus we should expect all subjects to label themselves as less fearful on a questionnaire, or when *thinking* about how fearful they are of snakes. However, on the basis of the goals of the different treatment procedures, we should expect the desensitized subjects to be less able to actually handle a snake than the modeling subjects, who have learned snakes are not harmful.

These two studies demonstrate quite clearly that (1) social learning techniques (modeling and desensitization) can greatly affect attitudes and overt, nonverbal behavior, and (2) changes in attitudes are not necessarily accompanied by changes in behavior. In social learning terms, the consequences of thinking about a feared object may be changed quite drastically without changing the consequences of overtly interacting with the feared object. A subject can say he does not fear talking in public when he is sitting alone in a room filling out a questionnaire, but when he is on a stage speaking in front of an audience, his reaction may be entirely different. Therefore, techniques designed to change only the way in which a subject talks about his behavior, or his feelings, will not necessarily produce changes in the subject's overt behavior or physiological reactions.

BEHAVIORAL SPECIFICITY AND GENERALITY RECONCEPTUALIZED

Now that a few of the principles of the social learning approach have been presented,[2] we can attempt to delineate how such an approach would recon-

---

[2] For a more extensive coverage of these principles see Mischel, 1968, or Bandura and Walters, 1963.

ceptualize attitude change research. In effect, this approach denies the utility of the concept of "attitude" altogether. What it does, instead, is discuss how different classes of behavior (one of which is self-ratings) are controlled by different sets of consequences (contingencies).

Let us see how this would explain the lack of consistency found in different measures of the same attitude. As a specific example, suppose that the attitude in question were, "birth control should be practiced." One measure of a person's attitude on this topic would be to ask him whether or not he agreed with this statement. Another measure might be the number of times this person, in fact, used birth control techniques. Chances are that if we were to record both these measurements, they would not correlate with each other. That is, people might say that they agreed with birth control, but they might not themselves use birth control techniques (as found in a survey of sexual behavior among Stanford undergraduates; see Chapter 1). A social learning approach explains this "inconsistent" result by assuming the following: people expect that verbally agreeing with the above state-ment about birth control will be followed by different consequences than actually not practicing birth control. The different consequences seem obvious. The important point here is that what seem, on an intuitive basis, to be measures of an underlying attitude toward birth control are, in fact, merely two different classes of behavior which are controlled, not by an attitude, but by the consequences of the behaviors.

When would the social learning approach expect verbal statements to match nonverbal behavior? Essentially, it would predict a match whenever a person expects similar consequences for both kinds of behavior, or (to put it another way) whenever he does not discriminate between the two kinds of behavior (or between their *consequences*).

Why should the previously discussed dissonance theory technique (in-ducing changes in *behavior* discrepant with an *attitude*) then lead to changes in the verbal behavior of self-ratings of liking, agreement, fear, etc.? One reason could be response-generalization. The subjects might generalize across responses, so that when one class of responses changes, the other class changes. Another, and more reasonable, possibility is that by engaging in unusual behavior (that is, counterattitudinal), a person is provided with a *new* set of experiences with the attitude object or person. For example, by getting a prejudiced person to talk to and interact with black people, he experiences a whole new set of stimulus-response-consequence relationships. If these consequences are more positive than those which he had expected, it is reasonable to assume that his feelings towards the stimulus (black people) should come into line with his new experiences and expectations. If we asked the person to describe his feelings, they should match this change, and thus be more positive. Another way to think about the dissonance technique is to imagine that the subject serves as his own model. That is, he sees how he, himself, is behaving in a new and different way toward the attitude object or person. The subject observes that he experiences a new set of consequences for the behavior in question. These new consequences then change the subject's future interactions with the attitude object or person. The reader may wish to develop for himself the ways in which this alternative hypothesis explains some of the dissonance theory experiments on "forced compliance" and justification.

In summary, a social learning approach discards the concept of attitude in its attempt to understand and produce changes in behavior. Instead, it determines the class of behavior that is to be changed (verbal, nonverbal, emotional responses, etc.). Then it tries to specify the "stuff" which the person has learned and which is therefore controlling his present behavior. Once these crucial bits of information have been found, the technique (modeling, direct reinforcements, persuasive communications, etc.) which is most likely to produce a change in such information is applied. Stated another way, by changing the expected consequences for engaging in the crucial behavior, or by changing the associations with a crucial stimulus, we can change *any* specific behavior, regardless of the general class to which that behavior belongs.[3]

In this chapter, we have discussed how to generate theories and techniques of attitude and behavior change by understanding and eliminating what appeared to be inconsistencies and inadequacies in experimental techniques and results. One theory (cognitive dissonance) was selected to illustrate how theories lead to new research and to new ideas about attitude change. By critically evaluating the theory, it was possible to derive insight into the conceptual and operational variables controlling attitude and behavior change. These new insights led to a possible reconceptualization of the whole notion of "attitude." From this reconceptualization came still further techniques for producing changes in verbal and nonverbal behavior. In conclusion, the simultaneous application of a critical and creative approach to experiments and theory has led us to generate ideas from which new techniques for solving practical problems can be derived.

---

[3] Research relevant to the application of the social-learning approach to practical problems can be found in the *Journal of Applied Behavioral Analysis.*

CHAPTER SIX

Focusing upon Practical Applications of Principles of Attitude and Behavior Change

We can now step out of the rarefied air of psychological theory and the purified atmosphere of the laboratory to look at relevant situations in our own lives. This does *not* mean that the behavioral sciences have already amassed a large enough body of reliable data or developed theories comprehensive enough to explain how variables interact to change attitudes. On the contrary, there is a real need both for better theory and more compelling data, but the practical problems facing us today demand an immediate solution. We must proceed with what we know, and hope that the scientific analysis of the attitude-change process will develop concurrently with the practical analysis of realistic concerns.

THE HISTORICAL FOUNDATION FOR A SCIENTIFIC APPROACH

The impetus for the systematic study of attitudes, which began in the 1940's, came from problems created by World War II. The problems were those of assessing the social-personal attitudes of bomber crews, evaluating the effects of persuasive films on soldiers, determining reactions of white soldiers toward Negro infantrymen in their division, getting housewives to change the food habits of their families, etc. In July of 1941, the Secretary of War issued an order that no surveys of attitudes of enlisted men could be undertaken because of their possible "destructive effect on morale." Nevertheless, a study was done the day after Pearl Harbor, and it showed that the evidence gathered from attitude questionnaires was much better in pointing out critical weaknesses in certain military practices than were the previously used officers' reports. The latter were impressions of a haphazardly selected, biased sample of informants—the worst kind of evidence. Stouffer (who headed a group of psychologists working for the Research Branch, Information and Education Division of the War Department), in his studies of the attitudes of American soldiers (1949), noted that relatively little use was made of controlled experiments to evaluate the effect of propaganda and changes in military procedures on attitudes. This was largely due to a lack of good criteria for evaluating when these subtle changes in attitude occurred.

A scientific approach to communication and attitude change developed directly out of this wartime research, under the direction of Carl Hovland. He had worked on experiments in mass communication (cf. Hovland, Lumsdaine & Sheffield, 1949) while in the army, and later inaugurated the Attitude Change Center at Yale University. The research which followed was aimed largely at a specification of the independent variables which might increase the persuasiveness of a communication, as well as at an elucidation of underlying psychological mechanisms and processes. However, the course of this research has in part reflected a general trend in the development of social psychology over the past two decades. There has been a movement away from studying "socially significant behavior," social problems, and social issues (thought to be the "bag" of the sociologist). The *content* of the attitudes has become irrelevant to the major concern. Independent variables and mediating processes have become the focus. Thus the attitude topics chosen for study, their measurement, and even the wording and construction of the persuasive communications are relegated to a position of minor concern. The only criteria typically used in their selection are ease of use and the hope that the topic chosen will allow large differences between groups as a function of the independent variable.

The pendulum is now moving back. Since events in our society are forcing social scientists to become involved with the way things really are, we believe that the time is ripe to wed the two approaches. For optimal progress, we must strive for a more vital and sophisticated *scientific* understanding of the principles of attitude change, while simultaneously trying to solve some of the *social problems* which are threatening to destroy our world.

In this concluding chapter, then, we want to examine a number of practical attempts to change attitudes and behavior—attempts which start out with a desired, often specific, goal in mind. In so doing, we will be espousing the problem-centered orientation we proposed right from the beginning of this book. In addition, we hope that the reader may begin to see how the applied and pure approaches may interact to the mutual benefit of both.

We now ask you to consider with us the following range of problems from which will be drawn practical, concrete illustrations of attitude and behavior change programs in action. Is "creating an image" a *new* Madison

Avenue approach? In what sense is our educational system a propaganda mill? What does psychological warfare propaganda look like, and how can it be detected? How can the prejudiced attitudes of a given woman toward a minority group be changed? How do businesses and advertisers trade on our unconscious motives to force impulsive buying? How can the police get you to change your attitude against self-incrimination, and thereby confess to a crime which may deprive you of your freedom or life? Finally, how can you get housewives to buy ready-made curtains in a country where window size is not standardized, or convince retailers to buy merchandise at a time when they have an adequate inventory, the currency has been devalued by fifty percent, and it is not the season for your product?

CREATING AN IMAGE, OR "PACKAGING" THE COMMUNICATOR

Although television has made us aware of the extensive use of public relation firms to promote the campaigns of political candidates, the basic technique was first used many years ago. An enterprising public relations man (whose pseudonym was Ivy Lee) was hired to change the prevailing stereotype of John D. Rockefeller, Sr. Mr. Rockefeller was generally considered a self-aggrandizing robber baron. A complete image reversal was called for, one in which the public would view him as a philanthropic, kindly gentleman. The strategy was deceptively simple; one of the most effective techniques was to publicize pictures and stories of Rockefeller giving shiny new dimes to every child he met in the streets.

EDUCATION: HIDDEN PROPAGANDA FOR THE ESTABLISHMENT?

Traditionally, propaganda is defined as an attempt to influence public opinion and public behavior through specialized techniques. It is contrasted with education, in which there is also an attempt to change attitudes and behavior but to do so through information, evidence, facts, and logical reasoning. In an ideal sense, educators teach students not *what* to think, but only *how* to think. In this way, the propagandist differs from the educator because he intentionally tries to bias what people see, think, and feel in the hope that they will adopt his viewpoint.

But are there concealed, subtle forms of indoctrination in education which cloud these neat distinctions? Think back to the examples used in your textbooks to teach you the purely objective, academic discipline of mathematics. Most of the work problems dealt with buying, selling, renting, working for wages, and computing interest. These examples not only reflect the system of economic capitalism in which the education takes place, but are an endorsement or legitimization of it. To illustrate, take an example which might be used to make concrete the arithmetic operations involved in the solution to: 90 divided by 60. "John wants to borrow $90, but Joe can only lend him $60. What percent of the amount he wanted does John obtain?" The same conceptual operations could be equally well learned with a different illustration, perhaps less likely in our country: "John earns $60 a week for his labor from Company X. Medical and health authorities are agreed that the weekly cost of living for a family of four is $90. What percent of a decent, acceptable minimal wage does Company X pay John?"

While such an example may seem farfetched, consider the complaints of the black community that textbooks in all areas omit reference in word or picture to the reality of black history, black culture, or even black existence—except as related to slavery and primitive native customs. Such an omission fosters the majority attitude upon the black child that his race (and he as a member of it) is insignificant. If this is not an intentional goal of our educational process, then its impact should be assessed, and correctives considered immediately.

PSYCHOLOGICAL WARFARE

The problem of comparing the concealed purpose of a communication to its obvious manifest content is one of the central tasks in analyzing propaganda used in psychological warfare (the organized use of propaganda, or nonviolent persuasion, against a military enemy). The purposes of such propaganda[1] are:

Conversionary, to weaken or change the emotional, ideological, or behavioral allegiance of individuals to their group (army, unit, village, nation, etc.);

Divisive, to split apart component subgroups of the enemy to reduce their combined effectiveness (the Allied propaganda tried to make German generals think of themselves first as Catholics; the Viet Cong propaganda stresses the subordinate status of blacks in America to create further dissension in the ranks);

Consolidating, to insure compliance of civilian populations in occupied zones;

Counteracting, to refute an effective theme in the propaganda of the enemy.

Examples of German Propaganda

The reader may imagine for himself how the morale of American soldiers might have been affected in World War II by studying the examples of German propaganda leaflets shown on the next three pages.

---

[1] See Linebarger, 1954.

WHAT TO DO

✝ REMEMBER, the Kreuzotter [pronounced CROYTS-otter] is about two feet long, dark grey in color, with small black crosses running the length of its body.

✝ IN THE DAYTIME avoid rocky areas where the Kreuzotter may be hiding. If you must walk among rocks, watch carefully for the snake, for it is well camouflaged. If you pass close to it, it may strike.

✝ AT NIGHT take all possible precautions to keep the Kreuzotter out of your tent. When you awaken in the morning, look around carefully, be sure it is not near before you get up.

✝ IF BITTEN do not get panicky. Do not run. Open the wound and bleed it immediately. If this is impossible, use a tourniquet. Send for aid at once.

WARNING

This is the Kreuzotter, Germany's only poisonous snake. During the daytime it is seldom seen. At night it becomes especially dangerous.

When the sun goes down the Kreuzotter goes in search of a warm place to sleep. Often it will coil next to a sleeping animal. When troops are in the field the Kreuzotter may crawl under a man's blankets or close to his sleeping-bag to keep warm.

In the morning, if the snake is disturbed, it may strike.

Maneuvers The Easy Way

The psychiatrists were right when they said life is what you make it.

Take this maneuver. It can be rough and miserable, or it can be a soft touch for any guy with an imagination.

For example, when you're standing around in the chow line waiting for cold salmon and beans, why make matters worse by griping about it.

GIVE YOURSELF A BREAK AND THINK ABOUT THE GOOD OLD DAYS.

Why Complain?

Instead of cold
salmon and beans

remind yourself about
a real mouthful,

Instead of grime and
mud in the field

Sunday dinner with fried chicken
mashed potatoes, cole slaw, cherry
pie

remember all those

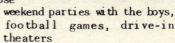

weekend parties with the boys,
football games, drive-in
theaters

Instead of night
guard and details

think about

Saturday night dates with
soft lights and soft shoulders -- and no curfews

**THIS MANEUVER SHOULDN'T GIVE YOU ANY TROUBLE
AT ALL. ALL YOU NEED IS A LITTLE IMAGINATION.**

PREJUDICE: HERE TO STAY?

Although the study of the techniques used to create and analyze such war propaganda is interesting and valuable, we hope that the use of these techniques will eventually be unnecessary. Perhaps some of the energy devoted to such "war games" can be brought to bear upon a problem of vast significance which is now dividing communities and nations, the problem of racial prejudice.

Racial, ethnic, and religious prejudice may be viewed as a negative evaluation, and as a rejection of an individual solely because of his membership in a particular group. If those discriminated against (as well as those who are prejudiced) suffer because of this prejudice, then why don't we eliminate it? Dedicated social scientists and humanitarians have been concerned with this problem for a number of years. The United Nations and the United States have spent millions of dollars on *information* campaigns to correct stereotypes about minority groups, to present the facts, and to help people to get to know one another. They assumed that prejudice was based on ignorance and that every man's desire to know the truth would dispel false beliefs. From every indication we have, these campaigns have been very limited in their effectiveness.

A second approach used to combat prejudiced attitudes has assumed that *contact,* or physical proximity between members of the groups in question, would make attitudes more favorable. For example, you take a class of white students on a tour of Harlem, or you mix races in a public housing project, at a summer camp, in an infantry outfit, or in the classroom.

There is some equivocal evidence that as long as the contact continues, the prejudiced attitudes may weaken, but there is little enduring or pervasive positive change in either prejudiced attitudes or discriminatory behavior.[2]

If these attitudes could be changed by some "correct" information and by intergroup contact, then prejudice should be minimal in a situation where both groups have equal power, available information, and favorable support for integration by the sponsoring organization. Such a situation should prevail in Northern municipal (tuition-free) colleges which have never been segregated and which admit blacks and whites solely on the basis of proven academic achievement. However, a study done by Zimbardo in

---

[2]In a real-life attitude change situation, one must consider not only whether the techniques used produce a big immediate change. What is vital is whether the change is maintained when the individual returns to the environment or group which supports the old behavior. Criminal recidivism and the return to drugs by "cured" drug addicts may be traced to "changed" individuals being sent back to an unchanged social setting in which their new attitudes and behavior are not socially supported.

1953 showed that in one such college there was a distinct pattern of self-segregation by black students (which was encouraged by the whites). Furthermore, a follow-up study showed that the pattern was still there ten years later, after a decade of civil rights legislation and presumed changes in prejudiced attitudes.

But enough of abstract arguments and experimental data. Judge for yourself whether information and contact are effective variables in changing prejudice. Here is a case study of a college freshman trying to persuade a middle-aged housewife that she holds untenable attitudes toward Puerto Ricans who were then (1954) moving into "her" East Bronx neighborhood. The woman has already had a great deal of contact with Puerto Ricans who live in her building, shop at the same stores (and own some of them), and are friends of her daughters. The boy provides sensible, rational arguments in favor of a general attitude of tolerance and understanding of the problems of this new group of migrants to the American Melting Pot. In reading this account of the transcript,[3] note not only the boy's efforts to change the woman's attitude, but also the techniques the woman uses to make her position convincing. Also, try to see beyond her rational manifest concern to notice the nature and the variety of topics she raises, especially those which come out when the boy has trapped her in an inconsistency.

Interviewer (P. Zimbardo): You've been living in this neighborhood quite a number of years. Do you think there's been any change in the composition of the neighborhood?

Woman: There certainly has. I've been living in this house now for 21 years, and I daresay I'm ashamed to tell people that I live in the neighborhood I do.

Boy: Why is that?

Woman: Because of what the Puerto Ricans have done to it.

Boy: What do you mean, specifically?

Woman: Well, to start with, their filth. Second, the language they use, and third, because the teachers waste eight hours a day with them in school and find that they get nowhere the minute the children are released.

Boy: You mean you never heard that language from anyone else but a Puerto Rican?

Woman: I certainly have, but not as much as I hear it from them.

Boy: Maybe you listen to it from them more often than you listen to it from others.

Woman: I can't help it, because the streets are overcrowded with them.

---

[3] A transcript of a tape recording made by Zimbardo in a community center in New York City. The participants agreed to talk about conditions in their neighborhood and were aware they were being recorded.

Boy: Well, why are they overcrowded with them?

Woman: It doesn't have to be overcrowded, they can live some-where else, or gather somewhere else. But I find that this is the biggest dope center, because there's nothing done about it. We pay police the salaries that we do, we pay taxes, and yet what has been done?

Boy: What do you know about dope centers? You say this is the biggest dope center. Do you know of other dope centers . . . . (Woman: I can't help but know, because I see it right under my window.) Do you know of other dope centers?

Woman: I don't look (Boy: So how could you say . . . .) but this is something you can't help but see.

Teenage Daughter (overlaps): You don't judge people all over the world, you judge people by your own neighborhood. If there are bad people right in your neighborhood, you don't say that every-body's bad or everybody's good, you judge by your own neighbor-hood . . . (Boy: Well, you're Jewish, right?) This happens to be a terrible neighborhood.

Boy: You're Jewish, right?

Daughter: Yes.

Boy: You don't know any people that are Jewish that are bad or that you wouldn't associate with?

Daughter: That's right, but they didn't tear down the Bronx like the Puerto Ricans did.

Boy: So you're going to say . . . are you gonna say that all the Jewish people are bad just because you know a few of them that you wouldn't associate with or you don't like?

Woman: I think they're the filthiest race, they're devoid of brains, and it's a disgrace with what goes on.

Boy: Why do you say they're the filthiest race?

Woman: They are, because I've worked with colored people, and I find that they're 50 percent more immaculate than the Puerto Ricans.

Boy: Well, why are they dirty? Isn't there a reason why they're dirty?

Woman: They don't know any better, unfortunately.

Boy: So then how can you condemn them because they don't know better? If you find a person that's ignorant, are you gonna condemn him?

Woman (overlaps): You can condemn people for being poor, but you can't condemn them for being filthy. [She means the opposite, or does she?] Soap and water doesn't cost much. If a person is ignorant, he knows nothing about cleanliness. And if he's devoid of brains, he certainly doesn't know.

Boy: All right, look, you say they're filthy and all that. But look at the sanitation problems in Puerto Rico.

Woman: I've never been to Puerto Rico, so I can't speak about Puerto Rico. I live in the Bronx and I can only tell you what happens there.

Boy (overlaps): In New York here or even in the United States we have the highest standard of living. They don't have that in other places, if a person just comes over from a low standard of living into a high standard of living . . .

Woman (interrupts): Why is it that most of the Puerto Ricans own the most beautiful cars, and yet 90 percent of them are on relief?

Boy: A lot of people own cars and don't have a lot of money.

Woman: Not a lot. Puerto Ricans more than any other race.

Boy: Why Puerto Ricans more than any other race?

Woman: 'Cause I happen to know someone that works on the Home Relief Bureau [Welfare Service]; and more Puerto Ricans than any other race.

Daughter: Why d'ya think they live so many in a family? They can't support children, they don't know how to bring 'em up, they haven't got the money . . . .

Woman: But they know how to make them, every nine months.

Boy: So are you going to condemn them for having kids?

Daughter: No, you don't condemn 'em, but if they don't know how to bring them up . . . .

Woman: Why do they have so many of them? *You could condemn them for having kids.* They should go out and look for jobs! The hospitals are flooded with them today. Do they know about going to pediatricians? No! Do they know how to raise children? No! What do they bring them up on? When the child's seven months old, it learns to drink beer from a can!

Boy (interrupts): My God, the people . . . the people just came over here, how long have they been in the United States? What chance have they had?

Woman: They've been here much too long to suit me.

Daughter: There are girls we have right here on our own block, little snot-noses, ten to twelve years old, hang out with these boys, they go in . . . they go up the schoolyards, they're, uh [becomes emotionally agitated] . . . at night when they should be home getting ready for school, gettin' ready for, uh, the next day . . . .

Boy: That's only Puerto Ricans, you don't know any . . . no other white girls or any thing like that?

Woman: It was never as obvious as it is now.

Daughter: No, all these girls are Puerto Ricans.

Boy: So you blame them for being *obvious* instead of hiding it . . . right? Instead of being sneaks about it?

Woman: Yes, because their parents don't know enough to take care of them.

Boy: How do you know their parents don't know?

Woman: Because if you go to dance halls, who do you find there? More Puerto Ricans.

Boy: You find anybody at dance halls . . . (Girl: Wait a minute, don't you think at the age of . . . .) You mean before the Puerto Ricans came there were no dance halls?

Woman: Refined, but not like now.

Boy: Why refined? What do you mean by . . . . You never read in the papers or anything like that where there were fights in dance halls where there wasn't Puerto Ricans?

Woman (interrupts): I lived in a building that was the most up-standing house on the block. Today it's disgraceful, because it's surrounded with Puerto Ricans.

Boy: Surrounded with . . . . Why? Do you think just because a person's Puerto Rican, right away he's filthy and he's dirty and he's dumb? You think just because a person's a Puerto Rican or something like that, that you call him dumb and ignorant because he's born Puerto Rican? A few years ago there was prejudice against the Jewish people. They weren't allowed in colleges, they're not allowed in colleges, they're not allowed in, uh . . .

Daughter (interrupting): And you have to be afraid to let, to let your children go . . .

Woman: Why is it that a family of ten moves into a three-room apartment?

Daughter: Because they're Puerto Ricans.

Boy (overlaps daughter): Answer me why. Because they like it?

Daughter (overlaps boy): Because they like to save money to buy cars.

Boy: They like to save money. Maybe they can't afford larger apartments.

Woman: Then they shouldn't come here. They should stay in Puerto Rico.

Boy: Is it so easy to find apartments now that you can go out and get all the apartments you want? So then why are you condemning?

Woman: It isn't easy, because I'm a little fussy. I want to stay away from them. I want to go to a neighborhood that *restricts them.*

Boy: But you still didn't answer a question I asked before. Just because the . . . they're Puerto Ricans or something like that, they're . . . that they're filthy, they're dirty. How many years ago was it before the Jewish people were, uh, discriminated against?

Woman: Not that I know of.

Boy: Not that you know of! How . . . a Jewish people . . . A Jewish person couldn't get into law school or anything like that then, you couldn't get into the Bell Telephone Company, you couldn't get into . . . to millions of jobs.

Woman: That's only hearsay. But can you prove it?

Boy: It isn't, yes, I can prove it. I have relatives that tried out for the Bell Telephone Company and they couldn't get in because they were Jewish. I had a . . . one of my relatives graduated from law school. He was one of the first people who graduated like that.

Daughter: So tell us why has the Bronx come down so much?

Boy: Because it's overpopulated.

Daughter: With dirty Spics!

Boy: So what reason do you have to call them dirty Spics?

Daughter: What reason!

Woman: One, because they don't know how to bring up children. Second, because their morale [she means morals] is so low. Third, because they're known to consume more alcohol than any other race in this world.

Boy: Aw, that's ridiculous. You never heard of Irish people drinking beer? Who drinks more beer than Irish people?

Woman: And fourth, they're the biggest marijuana smokers.

Boy: Who drinks more beer than Irish people?

Daughter: Yeah, but, uh . . . most Irish people can afford it. You walk into the house of Puerto Ricans and you find that under the bed people are dying, uh . . . their children haven't got clothes. Their children have no food . . . but you'll find beer cans under the bed.

Boy: Where did you ever walk into a house and see somebody under a bed? (laughing)

Woman: Who wanted to shoot the President, if not the Puerto Ricans? [reference to assassination attempt on President Truman by Puerto Rican Nationalists]

Boy: What about John Wilkes Booth, who tried to shoot Abraham Lincoln, what was he?

Woman: You're going back so many years!

Boy: All right, so what does that mean?

Woman: You pick up the paper and read about prostitutes. Who's involved? Puerto Ricans.

Interviewer: We seem to be going off on a tangent, so let's wind up the discussion with your views on how the problem could be solved.

Boy: About ten years ago we were the minority group, the Jews, and when we went to Jewish school the Irish used to pick on us. People find faults with the Puerto Ricans because they are the lowest and newest minority group now, and there's no real reason for that, actually it's ignorance, that's all prejudice really is, and it must be changed by getting to know them.

Woman: It could be solved by dropping a token in the subway and sending them all back where they came from!

The boy clearly had good intentions and worked hard to persuade the woman away from her anti-Puerto Rican position. He gave some sound arguments, refuted some of the opposing arguments, gave personal examples of prejudice toward him, and made a sincere appeal to view prejudice as ignorance which can be overcome by simply getting to know your disliked neighbors regardless of race, religion, or ethnic background. And to what effect? The woman exhibited a "boomerang" effect, reacting with more overt hostility and prejudice than she showed initially.

Good intentions unsupported by sound psychological knowledge may get the boy into heaven, but they will never change this woman's attitude. Where he failed was in not assessing the function her attitude serves in her total psychological makeup, and by accepting her rationalizations as rational statements.[4] The major consequence of the boy's puncturing one of her arguments, or directly confronting her with contrary evidence, was for her to become both emotionally upset (at points, both she and the daughter were near hysteria) and more openly hostile over the course of the interview. Her tactical reaction was to change the topic and regain her composure while the boy was shifting gears in order to reply to a nonsequitur which she had tossed off. Then she would attack again.

Our prejudiced woman is extremely concerned with order in her environment: she engages in pseudoscientific thinking (using apparently logical forms of rhetoric); she denies causal explanations of events, preferring to see states and attributes as given; she is "anti-intraceptive" in that she refuses to acknowledge any contrary information about herself or her views; finally,

---

[4]While there may have been a kernel of truth in some of her stereotypes, their validity is not the basis of her attitude toward the Puerto Ricans. It is likely that her prejudice is extended to all groups she considers to be inferior. Thus she would probably have the same negative evaluation of the Chinese in New York, regardless of the "information" she used to support her attitude.

she relies heavily on appeals to authority and hard "statistical facts" (which, incidentally, the boy never challenges). Of major significance, moreover, is the inference we may draw that a central preoccupation of this woman is sex. Her comments abound with sexual references, as does her daughter's over-reaction to the assumed sexual acts behind the schoolyard. Think of the underlying construct which might integrate the topics the woman raises: cleanliness and filth, morals, having babies, prostitution, the obviousness of what the teenagers do, dance halls, etc. It is instructive to compare the similarities between this woman's traits and those characterized as typical of the authoritarian women studied by Frenkel-Brunswick, Levinson, and Sanford (1958, p. 654).

A Customized Tailoring Job is Required

Using the functional approach to attitudes as suggested by Katz (1960), or a psychoanalytic approach as delineated by Irving Sarnoff (1954), one might say that her prejudiced attitudes served an ego-defensive function for her. They protect her from becoming aware of repressed conflicts which, if aroused, would create intense anxiety with which she could not cope. Her attitude, then, is a symptom of an underlying conflict which may be based on repressed hostility developed many years ago toward her father, or on repressed expression of her sexuality, or some similar causal agent.

If this analysis were accurate (and one would need more information to establish such a claim), then the inescapable conclusion is that the technique used to change her attitude must be tailored to the particular motivational basis upon which her attitude was formed. Trying to persuade her rationally only knocks out her props, attacks her symptoms, makes her more anxious as these defenses are weakened, and leaves nothing to replace them or to protect her against threatening thoughts about herself.

To change her attitudes, threats to her repressed impulses must be removed, conditions must be created to allow for emotional catharsis (support for a talking out of her problems), and self-insight should be developed through therapeutic techniques.

The intelligent reader will immediately see both the theoretical and practical limits to such a technique. Even if it were shown to be effective, it would require an individualized approach, much time, and considerable skill on the part of the therapist. How can it even make a dent in the statistically enormous problem facing us in the United States? Before giving up hope for a solution, let us describe an approach to attitude change which assumes that most behavior is unconsciously motivated. It can be applied on a large scale, and it appears to work.

MOTIVATION RESEARCH:
FOR HIDDEN MOTIVES, A HIDDEN PERSUADER

Ernest Dichter, the author of *Consumer Motivation* (1964), provides the keynote statement for us: "No successful advertising can ignore the stable, enduring attitudes of the consumer public. Since attitudes affect the way a product is seen, affect the very perception of facts, facts alone cannot combat hostile attitudes" (p. 396).

An entire industry, called motivational research, has developed from the assumptions that consumers respond to appeals which tap the irrational, emotional, and unconscious aspects of self.[5] This business uses a clinical, personality-oriented approach coupled with Gestalt psychology (which stresses the perceptual organization processes). The reactions of small groups of consumers to a specific product are studied intensively with depth interviews, projective tests, and free association tests. On the basis of these data and theoretical insights, motivation researchers claim that they can change the perception of potential consumers toward a product, alter attitudes toward it, and most important, get people to buy it. For businessmen, this is the only relevant criterion: does an advertising campaign result in increased sales? The reader might want to read Vance Packard's *Hidden Persuaders* for interesting examples and an evaluation of this approach.

Some of the problems worked on by people in motivation research are: how to get people to give blood to the Red Cross, how to design a one-minute television commercial with maximum impact, and how to increase airline ticket sales. Let us briefly examine how they do it.

It's Like Giving Blood

The appeal once made by the Red Cross to the patriotism of potential donors proved to be a dismal failure. This was because abstract, ideological principles rarely motivate immediate, concrete action. Using the skillful techniques of motivation research, it was determined that giving blood arouses many unconscious anxieties, especially with men, by whom it is equated with giving away part of their virility and strength. "There is a similarity between sacrifice, masochism, and feminine submission," says Dichter (p. 463).

If this is so, then information about the rapid regeneration of blood, or references to national emergencies will not be heard by the anxious individ-

---

[5]The reader should contrast these assumptions to the social learning approach briefly outlined at the end of Chapter 5. In doing so, he should note how a social learning approach conceptualizes changes in emotions and "unconscious" aspects of the self.

ual. Even if he acknowledges the truth of the facts, they will only raise the level of anxious conflict. While they increase his tendency to think about giving blood, they leave unchanged his unconscious tendency to avoid the threatening act. To get a man to give blood, then, it is vital to make him feel more masculine, to prove that he has so much virility he can afford to give away a little, and to make him personally proud of any suffering (for example, by giving him a pin in the form of a white drop of blood, the equivalent of a wounded soldier's Purple Heart Medal).

The relevance of this example to the issue of changing prejudiced attitudes based upon unconscious motives requires no comment other than that, in this particular instance, the recommended persuasive tactics did, in fact, result in a sudden, dramatic increase in blood donations to the Red Cross.

It's Like Giving . . .

If there is only a brief opportunity to expose a product, then (using the psychological principles of closure, the Zeigarnik effect, and active rehearsal) the way to design an advertisement for that time spot is to require the audience to concentrate on the task, to complete the task, and to rehearse the message *after* the direct exposure to it. Abbreviations like L.S.M.F.T. *(Lucky Strike Means Fine Tobacco)* are designed to meet these goals. Even more effective are the T.V. ads for *Salem* cigarettes in which the audience first learns a simple catchy musical refrain: "You can take *Salem* out of the country, *but* [pause] you can't take the country out of *Salem.*" Then at the end of the commercial, only the first part is sung, "You can take *Salem* out of the country, *but* . . . ." The listener will himself complete the pattern in order to gain closure. In so doing, he actively repeats the message.

An approach to the motivation underlying consumer attitudes can generate either specific tactics or a general strategy of approach. When a rationally designed advertising campaign to increase airplane ticket sales stressed the speed of the company's new jets, and described how quickly a businessman could get to City *X,* sales declined. Analysis revealed that this appeal stimulated guilt, because it described how fast a husband and father could get away from his family, perhaps for fun as well as business. On the basis of depth interviews, the appeal was changed to, "In only____hours you can *return* from your business trip in City *X* to your family." Sales rose sharply.

If the product being sold door-to-door by the Avon "ding-dong" sales-ladies were not skin beauty products, but rather a more tolerant attitude toward people whose skin color differs from the housewife, could we use these consumer motivation techniques to reduce prejudice and discrimination? It is worth considering.

HOW DO THE POLICE GET CONFESSIONS?

Recently in New York City, after intensive interrogation by the police, George Whitmore, Jr., gave a 61-page typewritten confession to the murder of two socialites. He was subsequently proved innocent. How can a man be made to incriminate himself like this when he knows he may forfeit his life as a result? If this occurs frequently, we must surely be dealing with a powerful set of attitude and behavior change techniques. As a matter of fact, about 80 percent of all arraigned suspects confess, after some period of police interrogation, to having committed a crime. While we do not feel that the police are always justified in using these techniques, we do feel that they are worth close examination.

Police interrogation has developed by trial and error over a long period of time, and the result has been a highly sophisticated array of techniques. They can be assigned to one or more of the following categories:

1. Demand characteristics of the interrogation environment. The environment is manipulated to create a given set or expectation in the suspect.

2. Perceptual and judgmental distortion. The suspect's perception of the crime is manipulated.

3. Distortion of the social psychological situation. The relationship between the interrogator and suspect is manipulated, and the social characteristics of the suspect are distorted to his disadvantage.

4. Utilization of personality and clinical psychology phenomena. The interrogator plays upon the suspect's personal motives and needs, and tries to establish a therapeutic relationship

5. Semantic and verbal distortion. Words charged with emotion or prejudice are used.

The Velvet Glove Approach

Psychology has replaced the physical abuses of the third degree, not only because the courts have made physically coerced confessions invalid, but also because the third degree is not as effective. "When you break a man by torture, he will always hate you. If you break him by your intelligence, he will always fear and respect you." (Kidd, p. 49)[6] This quotation comes from

---

[6]The techniques and quotations in this section come from:
1. Inbau, F. E., and J. E. Reid. *Lie Detection and Criminal Interrogation.* Baltimore: Williams & Wilkins, 1953.
2. Inbau, F. E., and J. E. Reid. *Criminal Interrogation and Confessions.* Baltimore: Williams & Wilkins, 1962.
3. Kidd, W. R. Police interrogation. *The Police Journal.* New York, 1940.
4. Mulbar, H. *Interrogation.* Springfield, Ill.: Thomas Publishing Co., 1951.
5. O'Hara, C. E. *Fundamentals of Criminal Investigation.* Springfield, Ill.: Thomas Publishing Co., 1956.

one of many police manuals which have been developed to transmit the most successful of the empirically developed interrogation techniques. The general approach of these manuals is expressed in the following excerpts:

> If one . . . has a layman's knowledge of practical psychology, and uses the salesman's approach, he can be successful in reaching into a man's brain and pulling out the facts he wants. (Mulbar, p. 5)

> For the last decade, candidates for a detective's post undergo an intensive six-week course that stresses the interrogation of prisoners. Most detectives, and especially the detective commanders, have a built-in psychology based on instinct and experience in which a man's weak points are exploited. They can get prisoners to talk as a result of this. (Michael Murphy, former New York Police Commissioner, quoted in *The New York Times*, November 7, 1963.)

Specific directions are given for fully controlling the interrogation and the suspect. The interrogator should be alone with the suspect, and "the full weight of his personality must be brought to bear on the emotional situation." He should sit or stand physically close to the subject, with no furniture intervening. He must possess no distracting mannerisms, and must never lose his composure. He can establish his authority by small gestures like prohibiting smoking, telling the suspect where to sit, or offering to get him a drink of water.

The interrogation should take place in an environment unfamiliar to the suspect. All psychological support from a familiar environment is thereby destroyed. The room should not be jail-like, but it should be quite sparsely furnished, quiet, and free of all internal and external distractions. There should not even be a telephone or ashtrays.

Confessions are often obtained by either minimizing the seriousness of the offense and allowing the suspect a face-saving out, or by using the opposite tactic of misrepresenting and exaggerating the seriousness of the crime.

Extenuation. The investigator says that he doesn't think the prisoner's indiscretion is too serious, since he's seen thousands of others in the same situation. Or he may shift the blame to circumstances (the environment, a subject's weaknesses, etc.). In either case, the prisoner may confess, feeling less guilty than he did before.

Misrepresentation. The interrogator might obtain a confession by misrepresenting facts, especially if the suspect is already emotionally confused. For example, he may falsely assert that he possesses certain incriminating evidence, thus making the suspect feel that the game is up and he may as well confess. The interrogator may use a "bluff on a split pair" to pretend, quite elaborately, that the suspect's partner has just confessed. Or he may put the accused in a fixed "reverse" lineup in which he is accused of a more serious crime than the one for which he was arraigned, and the suspect is grateful to be able to confess to only the lesser crime.

The friendly interrogator. There are several devices for making the prisoner feel that he wants to confide in the interrogator. For instance, the interrogator may flatter a suspect who feels socially insecure, or he may project an image of dignity and conservatism to prisoners who can be expected to admire these traits. He can pat the suspect on the shoulder, or offer to get him a Coke. If two interrogators are working in tandem, they can use the "Mutt and Jeff" technique in which one is very tough, while the other "protects" the suspect. If the tough interrogator subsequently leaves the room, the suspect may make a confession to the friendly interrogator.

These police manuals usually caution the interrogating officer that suspects should not be given the opportunity to deny their guilt. Experience has shown the police that the more often a person repeats a lie, the harder it becomes for him to tell the truth. Incidentally, this general principle was experimentally tested and verified in a laboratory experiment by Daryl Bem (1966). He demonstrated that when a person *lies* in the presence of cues previously associated with telling the truth (a "truth light" paired with true statements), he comes to believe in his false assertions.

AN ETHICAL QUESTION: WHO SUFFERS?

We are avoiding any editorializing about the moral or ethical value of any of these practical approaches to changing attitudes and behavior. They exist in our lives and are in constant use, to the advantage of some people and to the possible detriment of others. Those who object to these methods must first understand how and why they are so effective. The complexity of the problem of applying value judgments to different approaches is best illustrated in the next example.

Is it unethical to want people to brush their teeth or use mouth wash? Janis and Feshbach (1953) demonstrated that if an emotional appeal stimulates too much fear, its message will be rejected and little attitude change will be produced. We believe that this finding was the basis for an advertisement designed for a major pharmaceutical company. It first stimulated fear of regular oral hygiene treatments by a dentist, and then offered a less fearful alternative—using the company's mouthwash and toothbrush.

The headline declared: "Beware of Gum Disease!" It went on to state the symptoms of gum disease. If the reader had any of these symptoms then, "You ought to get to your dentist fast" [their underline for emphasis]. The ad then provided information about the action of bacteria. To the rhetorical question, "What can you do about it, you ask?", the ad gave an answer which ostensibly directed the reader to his dentist but, by describing a horribly painful, embarrassing dental experience, instead led the reader to question whether that trip was necessary.

> "Well, first of all, *have your dentist give you frequent oral hygiene treatments.* He can scrape away offending tartar and debris under which bacteria carry on their destructive work, damaging your gums and causing infections. Let your dentist also give you the benefit of prophylactic medication . . ."

The primary object of the advertisement (propaganda?) is then revealed: instead of going to the dentist, the reader and his family, in the secure comfort of their own home, can brush their teeth with brand *X* toothbrush and have a clean mouth and healthy teeth and gums simply by using brand *Y* mouthwash.

WHEN IT'S APRIL IN URUGUAY, ONLY SCIENCE SELLS CURTAINS

Changing any of the attitudes described in this chapter would be an easy task compared to the following challenge actually posed to one of our colleagues, Jacobo A. Varela, by an upholstery firm (Aerosol S.A.) in Montevideo, Uruguay. The firm's manager, Juan Diuk, and his assistants were trained by Varela to use social science techniques to solve the following problem.

Objectives: (a) To sell ready-made curtains to retailers; (b) to sell them both curtains and upholstery fabric in April (in order to reduce the wholesaler's inventory because new material was available at that time).

Difficulties: (a) The windows in Uruguay are not of standard size, so housewives have traditionally had their curtains custom made; (b) retailers have always bought new upholstery only in the spring (spring comes in September) because that is the time of year their customers buy material for spring home improvements.

Thus two well reinforced habits are operating against the influence attempt.

An almost insurmountable difficulty arose after the first planned program of change was completed (which will be described shortly). In an attempt to control a situation of spiraling inflation that had raised the cost of living by 90 percent in one year, the government froze all prices and wages, and devalued the currency to half its original worth. Severe penalties for infringements were established, and firms which violated these laws by raising prices were fined and their owners imprisoned. It is not surprising that virtually all nonessential consumer buying ceased. Likewise, buying by retailers from wholesalers came to a halt. Now imagine trying to convince a storekeeper who is uncertain and apprehensive, and who may still be overstocked from your previous persuasion attempt, that he should buy your new collection of upholstery.

We will only briefly describe the first April persuasion attempt (prior to the money devaluation which took place in June), in order to be able to develop in detail the second, more difficult, attempt.

The other approaches we have outlined so far have been based on experience, trial and error, clinical intuition, vague aspects of psychoanalytic theory, ingenuity, many implicit assumptions, and a smattering of low-level psychological principles. Although some of them have been successful, the success depended more on the particular person who was employing the techniques, or "practicing his art," than upon a sound social science base. With such a base, the control of behavior is predicated upon an understanding of the causal relations and, because it is explicitly spelled out, it can be implemented by anyone. The approach adopted by Varela tries to achieve this goal through the practical, systematic application of principles derived from psychological theories and especially from the results of social psychological experiments.

This approach begins by rejecting two of the criticisms often leveled against the possible utility of laboratory-experimental findings. How can you extrapolate from the laboratory to the real world when laboratory subjects are a captive audience in a novel environment which is under a high degree of control by the experimenter? And secondly (as we noted in Chapter 3), the time interval used in laboratory studies is rarely more than one hour, while in real life there is no such time constraint.

Instead of insisting upon bringing more of real life into the laboratory, this approach says that if laboratory studies are shown to be effective in changing attitudes (as Hovland, 1959, cogently argues), then bring the laboratory into real life. If an hour is enough to persuade an intelligent, often critical undergraduate subject, it should be enough to change the behavior of the average businessman or buyer, if a planned, concentrated, and powerful manipulation is used.

Persuasion Program One

Part A. The first problem was to lower the retailer's resistance against coming to the showroom, where it would be possible to show him the new items. Freedman and Fraser (1967) have shown that the probability of making an important commitment is increased if the person is previously induced to make a minor one. This "foot-in-the-door technique" was used in the following way: The salesman visited the store of the retailer (the target audience) and asked for a small favor: whether he would display a small sign which simply said, "Coming soon, Pronti-Cort." Since nothing further was explained to the storekeeper, his curiosity was piqued, and it was maintained by customers who asked him what the sign meant.

A week later, the salesman returned and asked those retailers who did the small favor to do a larger one—to come with him to the wholesaler's showroom, at which time the meaning of the sign would be made clear.

Part B. Most of the shopkeepers agreed, and when they arrived at the showroom, they were ushered into what was essentially an experimental laboratory. Stimuli in the showroom were displayed under optimal conditions, and responses of the buyers (e.g., facial expressions) were observed and recorded. To focus attention on the product (the ready-made curtains) and to hold it there, a visual presentation was made which used a combination of stimuli: color slides, a video tape movie of the prospective commercial, charts, room lights on and off at appropriate times, etc. Then an actual sample of the product, along with a persuasive description of its virtues and the advantages of new April sales, was presented to the store owner. Whenever his responses indicated that he was favorably impressed, he was asked to give his opinion about that product. To commit him to that favorable position, he was encouraged to elaborate on the reasons why he liked the sample. He was then immediately asked to make a further commitment by placing an order—which, with few exceptions, he did.

Part C. Another feature of this plan was not only to sell curtains but uncut fabric (yard goods) as well. This was done by using the technique of "distraction from persuasive intent" (described in Chapter 3). The fabric used in the pictures and in the sample curtains was very unusual, but no mention was made of it directly. Indirectly, the shopkeeper was made to compare these new textile designs with prosaic older ones. When he asked about the fabric, the salesman (with apparent hesitation in meeting this "demand" placed on him) agreed to show him bolts of the fabric. Once the retailer made this verbal commitment to see the material, and in addition put the salesman through the work of presenting it, he had to justify his behavior (see our discussion of Festinger's dissonance theory in Chapter 5). In such ways he very neatly *set himself up* for placing a big order.

Results. Normal September sales were about 30,000 units. The client hoped to sell 11,000 units in this April off-season attempt. After the persuasion attempt was designed, the experienced sales force optimistically estimated that 16,000 units would be possible. In fact, the actual sales for all retailers exposed to this persuasion series were 34,000 units! The wholesaler then trained the retailers to adapt these techniques to use in persuading their customers, the unsuspecting housewives with irregularly shaped windows. But once the government controls were effected (starting June 26, 1968), sales petered out until by September, when the new spring line of textiles was ready to be marketed, the buyers were not ready to buy any more.

Persuasion Program Two
Economic Depression in Springtime

The retailer is now expecting the salesman to return at this season of the year, and he knows from the past that the salesman wants to show him the entire collection of new styles (normally around thirty styles). But this time he is not going to buy!

The persuasion attempt that was used can be subdivided into several distinct stages within each of two parts:

Part A. In the retailer's store. During the first stage, it is necessary to change the businessman's verbal repertoire about business conditions in general. For example, he must stop saying, "Business is bad," and start saying, "Now is the time for business to pick up." Then one must get him to agree to a minimal commitment to see only a few new styles in the client's showroom.

Several weeks prior to this part of the process, a salesman stops by ostensibly to chat with the store owner, engages him in small talk, and then steers the conversation to business conditions, encouraging the store owner to make evaluative statements about business conditions and practices. The salesman thanks him for the interesting discussion, and then leaves armed with a list of the opinion statements which the storekeeper has made during their discussion.

From this list, six statements are chosen, varying in the degree to which the retailer (has said he) would agree with the positions they represent. For example, Statement I below is the one he would most endorse, while he also agrees with II and III. Statements IV and V are ones he disagrees with, and the final statement, VI, is the key opinion with which he disagrees. The objective of the persuasion attempt then is to change this last opinion, and to get the retailer to say (and to agree, rather than disagree) that "buying now is necessary." How can this be accomplished?

Statement	Customer's Initial Attitude
I. It is essential to keep up to date with new developments even in hard times.	+3
II. Varying the merchandise helps increase sales.	+2
III. The customary buying season is approaching.	+1
IV. The government will allow prices to be increased.	−1
V. Last year's collection sold well.	−2
VI. Buying *now* is necessary.	−3

The approach is interesting because the salesman encourages the storekeeper to disagree with him, to argue, and finally to reject statements made by the salesman. This works as follows. In stage two of the persuasion attempt, a different salesman visits the retailer and begins the conversation with reference to the first item. "Times are really bad, and *I* don't think it even pays to try to see what the new style trends are." The salesman says this as if he were trying hard to persuade the retailer to agree with his opinion. According to Brehm's theory of reactance, "the perception that a communication is attempting to influence will tend to be seen as a threat to one's freedom to decide for oneself" (1966, p.94). This is obviously a reverse use of manipulative intent, and is also the "Marc Antony effect." Accordingly, reactance is evoked by the salesman's obviously persuasive approach. In trying to reestablish his psychological freedom, the store owner rejects the influence attempt by saying that he would not go so far as all that, and that maybe it is only in idle business periods that one has the time to quietly study future trends. After the salesman gets him to elaborate and reaffirm his position on this point, he proceeds to disagree with the next statement in the prepared list. "Well, that may be true, but anyway, it would seem best not to vary merchandise too much in a period such as this." Again there will be reactance, with the store owner stating that, to the contrary, variety is the only thing that would give things a boost now. To this, the salesman replies that the retailer may be right, but that it doesn't matter anyway since they are not yet in the buying season. The retailer now reacts by saying that the season is definitely here. The salesman always eventually agrees with the shopkeeper after he verbalizes these opinions, thereby reinforcing the response of *disagreement.*

Now the salesman continues to disagree with statements which are only mildly disapproved of by the customer, like, "It might be the season, but the government will *not* allow prices to be increased." The store owner disagrees, argues against such a position, saying that the government *will* allow prices to be increased, and is reinforced in his arguments by the salesman. "Even if you could increase prices, you couldn't sell because last year's collection did not sell well." The retailer disagrees with this for two reasons: reactance and prior reinforcement in disagreement. Finally, the salesman moves to the statement with which the store owner initially most disagreed, "Well, even if last year's collection sold well, buying *now* is not necessary in order to make money." When the shop owner, now *set* to disagree, argues against this proposition also, he is in fact telling the salesman that he *ought* to buy now—exactly what the salesman wanted. His initial latitude of acceptance has been extended so that he now agrees with an extreme statement that he previously rejected (see our discussion in Chapter 4 of this attitude measurement technique of Hovland, Harvey, and Sherif, 1957).

By verbalizing these opinions, the customer tends to change his general attitude toward business and buying. He is left with the suggestion that, if he really feels the way he *says* he does, the salesman could try to arrange for a showing of only a few of the new styles. Typically, the self-convinced customer agrees to be shown new materials.

Part B. In the experimental showroom. Subsequently, the store owner is invited to come to the showroom with his wife, partner, salesman, etc. Selling is never done in the customer's store, since going to the showroom is the first act of yielding, involves some effort on the part of the customer (see Cohen, 1959, on the positive power of effort), and brings him into an unfamiliar environment which the salesman controls (reread the previously presented police confession techniques on this point).

In the first stage, the customer is given much attention and social approval of his views on a particular problem he is having in his business. The salesman looks into the eyes of the customer while agreeing with him. This intensive "eye contact" increases liking for the source of the approval (cf. Ellsworth and Carlsmith, 1968). Then he is shown some stock in a line that has made a small profit for him, but one which he is known not to be interested in at this time. When the customer finally says he came to see Line Z, Line Z is presented vividly and graphically.

As each design is presented, the salesman scans the expressions of the people in the group, looking for the one who shows most approval (e.g., head-nodding) of the design. He then asks that person for an opinion. Since the opinion is certain to be favorable, the person is asked to elaborate. As he does so, the salesman scans the faces of the other people, looking for more support. He then asks for an opinion of the next person now showing most approval. He continues until he reaches the person who initially showed most disapproval (who initially might have reacted negatively). In this way, by using the first person as a model (see Chapter 5), and by social group pressure on the last person, the salesman gets all or most of the people in the group to make a positive public statement about the design.

If the group includes a highly authoritarian owner accompanied by submissive subordinates, there will be a tendency for the subordinates to look to the boss before expressing an opinion. This is solved by seating the boss so that the subordinates cannot see his expression. The ensuing social pressure works on the boss even though it comes from subordinates, because often such a boss has a great need for social approval (cf. Crowne and Marlowe's analysis of social approval, 1960).

The final stage is now set. When it appears that the retailer might make a commitment to buy something, "immunity against counterpersuasion" is introduced (see McGuire's analysis of the importance of this technique, 1969). That is, there are two processes operating against the success of the company's persuasion attempt which must be counteracted. First, although the customer may be convinced that he ought to buy, he may be covertly generating counterarguments which would lead him to buy from the company's competitor. Secondly, even if he does buy now, he will face counterpersuasion from the competitor once out of the showroom. In order to get him to buy only from this company, and to establish the desired long-term commitment, it is necessary to make him immune to the competitor's appeals. How can this be accomplished in a short session?

The technique used is similar to that employed in the first part of the persuasion attempt: using a reactance technique and reinforcing the retailer for disagreeing with the salesman. In the first part, where the aim was to get him to have a more optimistic attitude toward business and buying, the method was to expand his *latitude of acceptance.* Here, the aim is to bring him around to a negative attitude toward Company *A* (the rival company) by expanding his *latitude of rejection.*

The customer has often bought from Company *A,* which is a very reputable firm that has high quality goods at reasonable prices with excellent payment terms. However, it makes few model changes and does not give exclusive lines. This last point is a source of irritation to many retailers, who do not wish to see the same goods that they are selling available at the lowest quality stores in lower-class sections of town.

The customer's initial attitudes toward the rival company are systematically manipulated by a combination of the reactance approach and the reinforcement approach. An example of how this technique can be employed follows:

(−3) Company A Gives Exclusive Lines

Salesman: [saying he liked a style in the customer's store and wonders whether Company *A* made it] Yes? Well, you are lucky to have that made *exclusively* for you!

Retailer: No, they don't give exclusives.

(−2) Company A Makes Frequent Style Changes

Salesman: [In an apparent defense of Company *A*]. You're right, that's too bad, but at least they make frequent style changes.

Retailer: Sorry, I must disagree, they rarely do.

(−1) Company A Is Very Regular in Deliveries

Salesman: Even if it is true that they don't (and I do believe you), you must admit that they make up for it by being regular and prompt in their deliveries.

Retailer: Here you're just wrong, they aren't so prompt, and their deliveries are often irregular.

(+1) Company A Offers Good Promotional Assistance

Salesman: That's surprising to hear, but judging from what I know of other companies, Company *A* is certainly good in promotional assistance, etc.

Retailer: [Now disagreeing mildly with a statement he previously would have agreed with] Well, sometimes they do, but you're not right if you mean they always do.

(+2) Company A Offers Very Favorable Terms

Salesman: Of course, *you* know better than I do about that, but I've heard that there's *no question* about the very favorable terms which Company *A* offers.

Retailer: I don't know where you get your information but there *is* some question about that issue; their terms are favorable to them, but not necessarily for the small shopowner.

(+3) Company A Is a Very Responsible Firm
[This is the "most accepted" statement which is to be modified.]

Salesman: You may be right, I never thought of it like that, but I am sure that you would *have to say* that Company *A* is a very responsible firm.

Retailer: [As actually happened in one case]. Not at all! They *used* to be a very responsible firm, but they aren't any longer!

In this way, the customer is guided not only to buy now, and to reject old loyalties to the opposition, but the general approach used is likely to engender a long-term commitment to the client, because he has not been forced to buy anything. Rather, the salesmen have been attentive, approving, reinforcing, concerned with his opinions, altruistic in saying nice things about their rivals—and they have allowed most of the work of persuasion to be done by the retailer himself.

TODAY TEXTILES, TOMORROW THE WORLD

Obviously, few of us are concerned about buying or selling textiles, but that is irrelevant to our discussion. The techniques and strategies derived from sound psychological research and theory should be equally applicable to problems that you consider to be socially significant and personally relevant. Your task is to use an approach like the textile sales campaign as a model for solving a problem whose content is meaningful to you—whether it be prejudice, cigarette smoking, birth control, political candidate preferences, or even trying to change the entire Establishment.

Suppose you as an individual, or as a member of a group in the minority, wanted to effect social and political reform in your country. Suppose further that you wanted to accomplish such a restructuring by "working within the system." You have at your command a set of powerful psychological principles and techniques for generating changes in political attitudes and behavior. Since systems and establishments represent nothing more than a conglomeration of individuals who share similar beliefs, opinions, and values (and means of defending them), the starting point of any psychological revolution is changing a single individual who is part of the system. In Postscript E we have outlined an approach to changing politically (or socially) significant attitudes.

We hope that this brief exposure to the area of attitude and behavior change will help you think more positively about the potential power you have to change others, and also about how to resist the constant attempts being made to change you. Before you begin any serious attempt to change others (in any direction), you must resolve for yourself the ethical question about the value and necessity of such change. You should also evaluate alternative proposals. This is as true for the educator and therapist as it is for the social reformer. Once you have decided to go ahead, then where you go and how you proceed ought to be determined by some of the considerations contained in these pages.

Techniques of Attitude Measurement

Several different paper-and-pencil tests have been developed to measure attitudes. Of these tests, four have been fairly highly refined and have been used most extensively. These major techniques are: Thurstone's method of equal-appearing intervals, Likert's method of summated ratings, Guttman's scalogram, and Osgood's semantic differential. A brief review of each of these methods will hopefully provide the reader with a clearer under-standing of how the social psychologist obtains the data from which he so elegantly extrapolates.

Each of the techniques to be discussed makes different assumptions about the nature of the test items that are used and the kind of information they provide about a person's attitudes. However, there are certain basic assumptions which are common to all of these methods. First of all, it is assumed that subjective attitudes can be measured by a quantitative tech-nique, so that each person's opinion can be represented by some numerical score. Secondly, all of these methods assume that a particular test item has the same meaning for all respondents, and thus a given response will be scored identically for everyone making it. Such assumptions may not always be justified, but as yet no measurement technique has been developed which does not include them.

THURSTONE'S METHOD OF EQUAL-APPEARING INTERVALS

The first major technique of attitude measurement was developed by Thurstone, in 1929, in his study of attitudes toward religion. The scale which he constructed introduced the metric to an area of research where it had never been used before. Thurstone assumed that one could obtain statements of opinion about a particular issue and could order them according to a dimension of expressed favorableness-unfavorableness towards the issue. Furthermore, the ordering of these statements could be such that there appeared to be an equal distance between adjacent statements on the continuum. Because of the latter assumption, one can make judgments about the degree of discrepancy between different people's attitudes. Thurstone also assumed that the statements are uncorrelated and that each statement has a position which is independent of the others. That is, acceptance of one statement does not necessarily imply the acceptance of any others.

A Thurstone scale is made up of about twenty independent statements of opinion about a particular issue. Each statement has a numerical scale value determined by its average judged position on the continuum. A person's *attitude* on the issue is measured by asking him to check those statements with which he agrees. His *score* is the mean scale value of those items which he checked. An example of a shortened version of such a scale follows:

Trait: Attitude toward open housing		
Scale value		Statement
Least favorable	1.5	A. A person should refuse to rent to anyone he doesn't like.
	3.0	B. Federal laws enforcing open housing should apply only to public housing, not to private neighborhoods.
	4.5	C. Local governments should publicly urge people to engage in fair housing practices.
	6.0	D. Only in extreme cases of discrimination in housing should there be some sort of legal intervention.
Most favorable	7.5	E. A person must rent to the first eligible applicant, regardless of race, color, or creed.

The hallmark of a Thurstone scale is that the intervals between the statements are approximately equal. This property of the scale is achieved by the method in which it is constructed. The first step is to collect a large number of opinion statements about some particular issue. Any statements which are confusing, ambiguous, double-barreled, or likely to be approved by individuals with opposed attitudes are immediately discarded. Each of the remaining statements is then sorted into one of eleven categories by a group of judges, according to the degree of favorableness or unfavorableness toward the issue expressed by the statement, *regardless* of the judges' own attitudes. These categories thus make up a scale which ranges from very favorable, through neutral, to extremely unfavorable opinions about the issue. By tabulating the ratings of all the judges, it is possible to calculate both the numerical scale position of each statement (its average scale value), as well as the extent to which the judges agreed in its placement (its spread of ratings). The statements which are selected for use on the final scale are those which have high interjudge agreement and which fall at relatively equally-spaced intervals along the continuum. A subject's attitude on the particular issue is then derived from his responses to this final set of scale items.

LIKERT'S METHOD OF SUMMATED RATINGS

One of the practical drawbacks of the Thurstone scale is that its construction is extremely laborious and time-consuming. To cope with this problem, Likert developed a different technique which could produce an equally reliable attitude scale with relative ease. The Likert scale is made up of a series of opinion statements about some issue. However, in contrast to the Thurstone scale, a person's attitude is measured by asking him to indicate the *extent* of his agreement or disagreement with each item. This is done by having the person rate each item on a five-point scale of response (strongly agree, agree, undecided, disagree, strongly disagree). A person's attitude score is the sum of his individual ratings. An example of a single scale item is the following:

A. "People should be allowed to move into any neighborhood they choose."

Rating value	
1	a) Strongly agree
2	b) Agree
3	c) Undecided
4	d) Disagree
5	e) Strongly disagree

Likert assumes that each statement that is used in the scale is a linear function of the same attitude dimension. This assumption is the basis for the operation of adding up a person's individual scores (or summating his ratings, to put it more formally) to obtain his final score. A further implication is that the items in a scale must be highly correlated with a common attribute and thus with each other, as opposed to Thurstone's distinct and independent items. It is important to note that at no point does Likert assume equal intervals between scale values. For example, it is quite possible that the difference between "agree" and "strongly agree" is much larger than the difference between "agree" and "undecided." This means that a Likert scale can provide information on the *ordering* of people's attitudes on a continuum, but it is unable to indicate how close or how far apart different attitudes might be.

Likert's method of scale construction is similar to Thurstone's in the initial collecting and editing of a variety of opinion statements. The remaining statements are then rated by a sample group of subjects on the five-point response scale in terms of their *own* opinions about the statements. This is in contrast to the Thurstone technique, where the ratings are made by trained judges and based not on personal opinions but on some relatively objective evaluation of where the statements fall on a continuum. The final Likert scale is composed of those items which best differentiate between sample subjects with the highest and lowest total scores.

GUTTMAN'S SCALOGRAM

A third scaling technique is based on the assumption that a single, unidimensional trait can be measured by a set of statements which are ordered along a continuum of "difficulty of acceptance." That is, the statements range from those which are easy for most people to accept to those which few persons would endorse. Such scale items are *cumulative,* since the acceptance of one item implies that the person accepts all those of lesser magnitude (those less difficult to accept). To the extent that this is true, one can predict a person's attitude towards other statements on the basis of knowing the most difficult item he will accept. An example of such a scale might be the following:

Trait: Attitude toward open housing	
Acceptability	Statement
Least difficult to accept	A. Generally speaking, people should be able to live anywhere they want.
	B. Real estate agencies should not discriminate against minority groups.
	C. The city should actively support the idea of open housing.
	D. There should be a local review board which would pass on cases of extreme discrimination in housing.
Most difficult to accept	E. There should be federal laws to enforce open housing.

In order to obtain a scale which represents a single dimension, Guttman presents sample subjects with an initial set of items and records the extent to which they respond to the items with specified answer patterns. These patterns, which are referred to as *scale types,* follow a certain step-like order. The subject may either accept none of the items in the set (score 0), accept item A only (score 1), accept items A and B only (score 2), accept items A, B, and C only (score 3), etc. If the subject gives a nonscale response pattern (e.g., accepts item C only and not those of lesser magnitude), it is assumed that he has made one or more response errors. By analyzing the number of response errors made, Guttman is able to determine the degree to which the initial set of items reflects a unidimensional attribute (that is, the extent to which they are "scalable"). The final scale is obtained by eliminating poor items and retesting sample subjects until a scalable set of items has been developed.

A person's attitude is then measured by having him check all the statements on the scale which are acceptable to him. His score is that of the appropriate scale type or (if he has given a nonscale response pattern) that of the scale type closest to his response. As the latter scoring procedure implies, it is almost impossible to develop a perfect unidimensional scale. This may be because people are actually responding not on the single dimension hypothesized, but rather on a different one, or on multiple dimensions.

OSGOOD'S SEMANTIC DIFFERENTIAL

The three methods just described attempt to measure attitudes by having people indicate the extent of their agreement with various opinion statements. In contrast to this approach, Osgood has studied attitudes by focusing on the *meaning* that people give to a word or concept. Underlying this technique is the basic assumption of a hypothetical semantic space of an unknown number of dimensions, in which the meaning of any word or concept can be represented as a particular point. Osgood's procedure is to have people judge a particular concept on a set of semantic scales. These scales are defined by verbal opposites with a mid-point of neutrality, and are usually composed of seven discriminable steps. For example, a particular person's meaning of the concept "integration" is measured by his ratings of it on a set of semantic scales:

good ___ ___ ___ ___ ___ ___ ___ bad

strong ___ ___ ___ ___ ___ ___ ___ weak

fast ___ ___ ___ ___ ___ ___ ___ slow

active ___ ___ ___ ___ ___ ___ ___ passive

and so on.

An analysis of the ratings collected by this method may reveal the particular dimensions which people use to qualify their experience, the types of concepts that are regarded as similar or different in meaning, and the intensity of the meaning given to a particular concept. Osgood's own research has indicated that there are three dominant, independent dimensions which people use in judging concepts. He refers to these dimensions as the evaluative factor (e.g., good-bad), the potency factor (e.g., strong-weak), and the activity factor (e.g., active-passive). Although this method can provide a lot of information about a concept, it is not exactly clear how the concept's *meaning* for a person is related to opinion statements he would make about it.

The Experiment as a
Source of Information

In psychology all research involves making observations of behavior. Some research, called field research, observes phenomena or the operation of variables as they exist naturally. That is, the researcher attempts to make systematic, relatively objective, and unbiased observations of things "as they are." He does not interfere with their functioning, nor does he try to change or control any of the variables. Indeed, his major problem may be that his very presence changes the behavior being observed (the psychological equivalent of Heisenberg's indeterminacy principle in physics). His task is to establish whether, and to what degree, sets of variables are co-related. For example, one field researcher showed that college girls at Bennington College in Vermont became increasingly liberal in their political and social attitudes from freshman to senior year. Another field study demonstrated that prejudice decreases with increased personal contact between Negro and white housewives in a housing project. Studies such as these are valuable in locating significant problem areas, describing and analyzing interesting behavioral phenomena, and in suggesting variables which might play a vital role in the relationships obtained.

Attitude surveys and polls form one subclass of observational research. However, regardless of the care, effort, and skill that goes into such studies, they are severely limited in the kind of information they can provide. A correlational study can never yield unequivocal conclusions about the nature of the *causal* relationships involved. Two events or behaviors may be highly correlated,[1] yet we might not be certain whether *A* caused *B*, or *B* caused *A*, or the relation was coincidental, or one indirectly caused the other through the operation of an intermediate (unknown variable), or whether a third variable caused the occurrence of both *A* and *B*, etc. These arguments are not mere academic exercises, and in fact they form the basis of the reply of the statisticians working for cigarette companies to the statisticians of the American Cancer Society regarding the correlational evidence supporting the smoking-cancer link. (The reader is referred, specifically, to the skillful reply of E. Cuyler Hammond, Smoking and death rates—a riddle in cause and effect, *American Scientist*, **46**, No. 4, 1958, pp. 331-354.)

In contrast to this naturalistic field research stands the experiment. An experiment simply represents a special way of making observations which, under appropriate conditions, allows for its conclusions to be statements of causality. It is only on the basis of such conclusions that a science of psychology can meaningfully approach its goals of prediction and control of behavior.

The researcher systematically varies one set of conditions (stimulus events) while attempting to exercise control over all others to which his subjects might be responsive but which are irrelevant for testing his particular hypothesis (an idea about how two or more variables are related). As he manipulates or induces change in these independent variables, he observes a small subset of behavior thought to be related to the known changes in the stimulus events. The experimenter does not wait for the behavior to occur naturally; he creates the conditions which he believes will elicit its occurrence. In this sense, he creates an artificial environment or interferes with a natural process. He does so in order to: (a) make the event occur under known conditions which can be independently replicated on subsequent occasions; (b) make it occur when the experimenter is prepared to make accurate observations (of the dependent variables); and (c) make it possible to establish causality, i.e., the direction and magnitude of the effect which the independent variable has upon the dependent one.

An experiment begins with three basic decisions. From among the infinite array of stimuli which a variety of subjects could perceive and respond

---

[1] When the variation in one set of data is related to the variation in a corresponding second set (e.g., 2 test scores for each person), the conclusion can be expressed mathematically as the coefficient of correlation, or *r*. This value may range from -1.0 through 0 to $+1.0$. When $r = 0$, the two distributions of data bear no relation to each other. Likewise, values which approach zero reveal a lack of systematic relationship between the sets of data. A positive value of *r* indicates that variation in each set of data is in a common direction; as *A* increases, so does *B*. A negative value of *r* indicates that *A* and *B* go in opposite directions. As *r* approaches either $+1.0$ or -1.0, it becomes more likely to predict one event knowing the other, that is, to explain the variation in one set of observations from knowledge of the variation in the other.

to at many levels in numerous dimensions, a specific stimulus, organism (or subject), and response mode have to be selected. An experiment can be conceived graphically as a set of three overlapping circles representing the population of all (a) stimuli, (b) organisms, and (c) responses relevant to the general problem under investigation. What the researcher studies is the very small area or point of their intersection. For example, in a study of the effects of light intensity on reaction time, the stimulus variable might be two levels of illumination; the subjects, 20 college male sophomores taking a particular course at a given college; and the response, lifting the right index finger off an electrically wired key.

Three general problems immediately spring to mind from this example: (a) is the response measure reliable, and is the obtained relationship a reliable one, (b) are these specific, concrete operations valid translations of the conceptual, abstract concepts of light intensity and reaction time, and (c) are the results generalizable to other classes of subjects, stimuli, and responses.

Reliability when used in this sense can be equated with consistency or stability. Will the response measure yield the same value on repeated occasions if the stimulus conditions are the same, or can the same results be obtained under different but similar circumstances of testing?

Validity is a more complex issue to demonstrate, and has several meanings, only a few of which will be mentioned. *Conceptual validity* implies that the treatments, observations, and measurements made by the experimenter are adequate concrete representations of the broader abstract class which the experimenter really wants to learn something about. He is interested in reaction time, not index finger elevation; or in attitudes, and not a check mark on a 10-point questionnaire scale. Ideally, what is desired is a specific set of operations which anchors the abstract concept to events in the real world, but is at the same time as pure an instance of the concept as possible.

Predictive validity describes the condition in which one may predict, from knowledge of a specific behavior, a second, operationally different but conceptually related behavior. For example, one can predict academic success in college on the basis of college board scores, or reaction times in highway driving on the basis of reaction test scores.

Validity can also be thought of in another way. First, we assume that any variation in test scores has two components: true variance and error variance. As the obtained score is closer to the (hypothetical) true score, it becomes a more valid measure. As its variation is influenced by variation not only in the relevant response being studied, but also by extraneous sources of error, it loses its status as a valid representation of the underlying true response system. *Systematic errors* bias the score in a given direction, while *random errors* can cause the score to deviate from its true value in any direction.

These omnipresent sources of error are the barriers to be overcome in attempting to uncover orderly relationships in the "booming, buzzing world of confusion" around us. Systematic errors may arise when the experimenter unintentionally gives the subject cues as to when the stimulus will be presented, or when an experimenter who knows which subject received a given treatment (e.g., a drug) is also responsible for making subjective ratings of his behavior. Random errors result from environmental disturbances or methodological inadequacies. A transient or irregularly occurring event could alter the true response to the manipulated stimulus on any given occasion (as when an unexpected noise occurs during a conditioning procedure). Similarly, the true score could be elevated or depressed in unsystematic and unknown ways if the experimenter presents the stimulus differently to each subject within the same condition, or else has not established an explicit criterion for measuring the presence or quality of a response. Systematic errors may be minimized by use of controlled procedures, objective scoring methods, randomization, and control groups. Elimination of random errors depends largely upon standard methodology and use of an environment not subject to random changes in features which could affect the subject's response.

To recast the goal of research in light of this present discussion, we might say that an experiment is a set of objective procedures for isolating a signal from a background of noise. The true score, or signal, must be conceptually purified to distinguish it from similar signals. The treatment procedures are designed to amplify the signal, while the measurement procedures should be able to detect even a weak signal. This is possible only when adequate control can be exercised over competing signals and background noise, either by minimizing them or by being able to precisely evaluate their contribution to the observed value of the primary signal.

But what about the generalizability of the findings of an experiment? Few scientists are satisfied with conclusions limited to the details of the specific operations used on a unique sample of subjects who gave a particular response. We want our conclusions to be at a higher level of abstraction. The extent to which one is willing to generalize from a single experiment to broad statements about stimuli, organisms, and responses is in part related to the state of knowledge in the specific area, the researcher's personal willingness to take risks, and his commitment to either a theoretical or a primarily empirical approach. However, we shall soon see that this process of inference is not as subjective as it might seem. In fact, there are rather precise statistical means for drawing inferences from the little a researcher has observed and applying them to larger, unobserved populations.

Before describing such procedures, we should mention the important function in experiments served by the technique of *random assignment* of subjects to treatment conditions. In order to be able to say treatment *A* had a greater effect on a given behavior than did treatment *B,* we must assume that the subjects were not different before exposure to the treatment variable. One way of achieving this goal is by selecting subjects in such a way that it is equally likely that a subject might be in the experimental treatment group or in the nontreatment control group. If assignment to a given condition is based solely on a chance procedure (e.g., toss of a coin, or use of a table of random numbers[2]), it usually insures that any of the multitude of organismic factors which might influence the results are equally distributed among the treatment cells prior to exposure to the independent variable. For example, random assignment would generally produce equal numbers of males and females in each condition. This process enables one to make statements of causality, as well as generalizations beyond the limited population studied.

There is always a risk involved in making inferences from a study, even if it is well-designed and carefully executed. However, the extent of this risk can be precisely calculated by means of statistically objective procedures which evaluate the probability that a given conclusion from a particular set of observations may be false. Suppose we wished to evaluate whether a given communication changed attitudes toward drug addiction. We might present the speech to a group of people whose opinions we had measured before, and again after, their exposure to it. The opinion scale ratings of our sample of subjects would first be summarized in a convenient and efficient manner by certain *descriptive statistics.* "What is the typical or average score before the communication, and what after?" is a question answerable by computing means, medians, or modes. "How much do individual subjects deviate from this representative value?" can be answered by establishing the variability of response (the range, or the standard deviation).

However, in order to determine whether it was the exposure to the communication which changed attitudes in the direction advocated, it is necessary to compare the obtained descriptive statistics with the estimated change which might have occurred from the mere act of repeated measurement of opinions, in the absence of the communication. Comparison of the obtained distribution of scores with different types of theoretical distributions allows one to estimate the probability that the data are not due to chance but to a statistically reliable relationship *(inferential statistics).* Different behavior (between groups of initially comparable subjects) in response to the treatment variable is more likely to be a "real" difference, as a direct function of three factors: number of observations, magnitude of the difference, and variability of the response. An obtained difference is more likely to be a significant one as the number (N) of observations increases, as the average difference between groups in performance is greater, and as

---

[2] A process by which all subjects are first given a number and are then distributed into the various cells in the research design according to a pattern determined by the appearance of their number among a larger set of randomly generated numbers.

there is more variation between different groups than there is within each separate group.

The concept of *significance* is defined in psychology as the minimum criterion for establishing that a given result is due to treatment effects rather than chance fluctuation (error variance) in the observations. A probability level, arbitrarily set at $p < .05$ (p is less than .05, or 5 percent), is this minimum standard. This means that the difference found would occur only five times in 100 by chance alone. Therefore, we may infer that this occasion is one of the other 95 times when the difference is not attributable to chance. Under certain circumstances, the researcher may demand a more stringent rejection probability, such as $p < .01$ or even $p < .001$ (i.e., only one time in 1000 will the experimenter draw a false conclusion by accepting his obtained difference as a real one).

Although the risk involved in drawing an inference is reduced by couching the conclusion in probabilistic rather than absolute terms, there is still considerable risk involved in making inferences in either of two directions from the sample of behavior observed. One can make inferences upward to a more abstract, conceptual level of explanation, or downward to a more concrete, specific instance. In the former case, there may be an error in extrapolation, in that the particular results do not reveal the presumed general relationship or theoretical process. In the latter, there is the problem of assuming that a general relationship can predict a specific person's behavior.

For each of these cases there are two types of errors possible. If the significance of an obtained difference is $p < .05$, then the experimenter will be wrong five times in 100 when he concludes that he has found a real effect. This is because chance alone can generate differences of the magnitude he has observed, and a particular experiment may represent one of those five possible chance occurrences. Here we have a type 1 (or alpha) error: inferring that a relationship exists when it does not. Looking at our probability and decision-making process differently, suppose the significance of a difference is rejected because it is at the .06 level of probability (beyond the conventional limit of scientific acceptability). Then 94 times out of 100 the investigator will conclude that no relationship exists when, to the contrary, it does. This is a type 2 (or beta) error.

How does the psychologist decide whether to be more risky (type 1 error) or more conservative (type 2 error)? Clearly, his strategy should be determined by the action implications of each type of conclusion, by the relative costs or dangers of each type of error, and finally by the stimulation or inhibition of creative thinking each may cause. For example, in making upward inferences to generate conceptual, theoretical statements about physical or psychological reality, progress may be more impaired by making a type 2 error (which could serve to close off an area of investigation prematurely) than by making a type 1 error (which ought to be readily discovered by others in independent replications). However, if replication studies are rare, then a type 1 error may be perpetuated, resulting in much wasted effort testing derivatives of the original, unsubstantiated hypothesis.

What faces the experimentalist is the dilemma of gaining control while losing power. The full range and intensity of psychological variables can only be approximated in the laboratory setting. This is because there is only a relatively brief exposure to the stimulus in an experiment. The subject's task is often of limited relevance to his other life experiences and has minimal implications for his future functioning. In addition, the nature and intensity of the experimental manipulations are limited by legal, ethical, and moral considerations. But while the power of variables is often best demonstrated under uncontrolled natural circumstances, studying phenomena at this level risks a loss of understanding of the processes involved, lack of specification of causality, and inability to analyze the complex network of factors into relevant component variables. On the other hand, the gains achieved by the superior control of an experiment may be offset by its trivial content. As a result of purifying, standardizing, controlling, and selecting certain stimulus and response dimensions, the experimenter may have created a very distant, watered-down version of the phenomena or problems he set out to study. Under such conditions the results of the investigation may have no practical significance, since it is not possible to extrapolate from them to action-oriented problems.

Sources of Invalidity
and Experimental Designs

The purpose of this postscript is first to give the reader some idea of the sources of invalidity possible in experimental research in psychology in general and in attitude change specifically, and then to present the reader with what are now considered to be the best available experimental designs, ones which are relatively free from errors.

There are essentially two sources of invalidity possible in an experiment. One kind of invalidity (internal) arises when conditions within the experiment prevent the experimenter from being able to draw any inferences about the hypothesis. The other kind of invalidity (external) arises when the experimenter tries to generalize beyond the results of a single experiment to events and people not included in the actual experiment.

Let us first consider what some of the sources of *internal invalidity* might be.

1) Internal artifacts. It is possible that an uncontrolled event which the experimenter did not want to occur caused the effect the experimenter observed. If this happened, a conclusion by the experimenter that *his* operations were causing the effect would be incorrect.

2) Subject changes. Rather than stimulus events (the independent variable) occurring outside of the subject, it is possible that they occurred inside of him. For example, the subject may have been sick, or worried about a personal problem.

---

[1] This postscript is largely derived from a book by Campbell and Stanley (1963).

3) Testing sensitization. Taking an initial test (premeasure) may affect how the subject reacts to a second test (postmeasure).

4) Problems with equipment. The equipment used in the experiment may change as a function of use or time.

5) Subject selection biases. If subjects are not assigned to experimental groups at *random* then there is always a chance that differences between experimental groups are caused not by differences in the independent variable, but rather by preexisting differences between the subjects in the various groups (as described in Postscript B).

6) Attrition. If, after subjects have been randomly assigned to conditions, an uncontrollable factor eliminates some of the subjects from the final analysis of the results, valid conclusions about the effect of the independent variable on the dependent variable cannot be drawn. One uncontrolled factor might be the subject's choice not to continue in the experiment. Another might be some feature inherent in the experiment itself.

Sources of *external validity,* or the generalizability of the experimental result, are:

1) Reactive effects of measurement. When subjects are given a test, say a self-rating attitude scale, it may be that taking the test itself influences how the subject will behave. In the attitude measurement example, the test may become the stimulus condition which elicits the attitude; either the subject did not have the attitude before, or he changes his true response after realizing the intent of the test or experiment.

2) Interaction of selection bias and experimental variable. The effect of an experimental variable may show up only on certain kinds of subjects. For example, if only subjects with extreme attitudes were studied, it is possible that variables which normally change the attitudes of more moderate subjects would not have an effect on these extreme ones.

3) Reactive effects of experiment. Specific differences between the conditions existing in the experimental setting and the conditions existing outside of it may be crucial in determining whether or not the results of the experiment can be applied. For example, experimental subjects might always be highly motivated to attend to the communication, a condition which would not occur naturally. It is obviously very important, in a practical approach, that this condition be noted in the experiments from which the change program is devised.

4) Multiple treatment effects. Sometimes each subject is measured with and without the experimental variable present. It is thus possible for sequential effects to occur; that is, the first manipulation affects how the second manipulation will influence the subject's behavior.

Now that we have presented a few of the more common sources of invalidity, let us see how well these sources of error can be eliminated by various experimental designs.

Table C presents, in summary form, a set of five highly sophisticated experimental designs. The symbol O in the table refers to observation or measurement, while the symbol M is used to refer to an experimental manipulation which is presented in that condition. In each of these experiments there are at least two groups of subjects. Some of the subjects experience the manipulation; others do not. Those subjects who experience the manipulation and those who do not are always determined randomly. This random assignment of subjects to conditions is indicated by an R in front of each group. So, for example, the simplest design presented in Table C is a two-group design

| Group 1 | R | M | O |
| Group 2 | R | | O |

in which the subjects are randomly assigned to one or the other group. Only subjects in group 1 experience the manipulation, after which both groups are observed.

Also in the table is a list of the various sources of invalidity previously described. For each design, if a "yes" appears in the column for the particular source of invalidity, it means that the design is not able to remove that particular kind of error. A "no" means that it does not have that problem.

The "best" design to use to minimize sources of artifact (error variance) is the Separate Sample Pretest-Posttest design. Here the experimenter randomly assigns subjects to a number of conditions. The experimenter initially measures the pre-treatment responses of only half of all his subjects. The remaining half is measured some time later. However, those subjects who are measured later are also divided in half so that one group experiences the manipulation and the other does not. Furthermore, the reader should note a very distinctive feature of this design. It is possible to demonstrate that the conceptual status of the independent variable is not limited to a single set of specific operations. By using two different sets of operations (M_1 and M_2), both derived from the same conceptual independent variable, general conclusions can be drawn from concrete observations to abstract variables.

In summary, some subjects are measured early, some later. Of those who are measured later, some get a manipulation, others do not. Of those subjects who experience a manipulation, some experience one form of it, while others experience a different one. Furthermore, different measurement techniques are used, and for each measurement technique some subjects experience, and others do not, each of the manipulations.

From this description the reader can see that, in any design, randomization is very important. It is also important that the *observations* made of the subjects do not interfere with the behavioral effects of the experimental *manipulations*.

TABLE C

Some Experimental Designs which Minimize Sources of Invalidity

Experimental designs	Internal sources						External sources			
	1. External artifacts	2. Subject changes	3. Testing sensitization	4. Problems with equipment	5. Subject selection biases	6. Attrition	1. Reactive measurements	2. Interaction of selection biases and experimental variable	3. Reactive effects of experiment	4. Multiple treatment effects
1. *Pretest-posttest design* Group 1 R O O 2 R O M O	No	No	No	No	No	No	Yes	Maybe	Maybe	No
2. *Solomon four-group design* Group 1 R O M O 2 R O O 3 R M O 4 R O	No	No	No	No	No	No	No	Maybe	Maybe	No
3. *Posttest-only design* Group 1 R M O 2 R O	No	No	No	No	No	No	No	Maybe	Maybe	No

TABLE C Continued

	Internal sources						External sources			
	1	2	3	4	5	6	1	2	3	4
4. *Time series with control*	No	No	No	No	No	No	Yes	No	Maybe	No
5. *Separate sample pretest-posttest design*	No	No	No	No	No	No	No	No	No	No

4. *Time series with control*

Group: Time →

1 R OOOOOOO
2 R OOOMOOO

5. *Separate sample pretest-posttest design*

Group

$\left. \begin{array}{l} 1 \\ 2 \end{array} \right\}$ R* $\begin{array}{l} \text{R O} \\ \text{R } M_1 \text{ O} \end{array}$

$\left. \begin{array}{l} 3 \\ 4 \end{array} \right\}$ R* $\begin{array}{l} \text{R O} \\ \text{R   O} \end{array}$

$\left. \begin{array}{l} 5 \\ 6 \end{array} \right\}$ R* $\begin{array}{l} \text{R O} \\ \text{R } M_2 \text{ O} \end{array}$

$\left. \begin{array}{l} 7 \\ 8 \end{array} \right\}$ R* $\begin{array}{l} \text{R O} \\ \text{R   O} \end{array}$

*Here one randomizes both by assignment of individuals to groups and by whether or not comparison groups experience the manipulation.

An Efficient Method
for Outlining Experiments

One of the general problems facing anyone wanting to get information from journals in psychology is how to read the various articles so that maximum information is obtained in the least time. To aid the reader in his organization of the literature, to increase his understanding and retention, and to assist in subsequent information retrieval the following outline can be used as an aid.

1. Title

2. Author(s)

3. Source and pages

4. Date performed

5. General problem area, e.g., prejudice, rumor, conformity, etc.

6. Reason for interest in the problem, i.e., why this experiment was done (e.g., contradictory results from previous studies, an observation of an interesting phenomenon to solve some practical problem, test of a formal theory or model, correction of previously poorly run study, etc.). Part of the reason for noting the experimenter's purpose is to determine whether or not the particular experiment(s) fulfilled its purpose.

7. What was the hypothesis(ses)? Here the reader notes whether or not a hypothesis is in fact stated or being tested at all. Furthermore, at what conceptual level is the hypothesis stated, i.e., at the concrete operational level or at a more abstract level?

8. What subjects were used, e.g., how many, sex, age? Did they have any special characteristics which might make the results from the particular study less generalizable to people without that characteristic? How were the subjects selected, i.e., volunteer, chosen at random, or matched on the basis of some characteristic such as intelligence?

9. Procedure
    a. Refer back to the hypothesis (if this . . . then that), and see how the "this" and "that" are operationalized in the study.
    b. How is the dependent ("that") variable(s) operationalized?
    c. How is the independent ("this") variable(s) operationalized?
    d. Are there any control groups? What is the function of each? Are necessary control groups missing?
    e. What about methodological control groups (for order, for fatigue, for experimenter bias, etc.)?
    f. Is there a deception? What is the subject's view rather than the experimenter's view of the experiment? How do they compare?

10. Results
    a. State major results and conclusions in terms of original hypotheses.
    b. What are the statistical significance levels of the results? (See Postscript B.)
    c. Are the statistical comparisons appropriate for the hypotheses stated?
    d. Are there any unexpected findings (i.e., results which go beyond the original hypothesis or limited focus of the initial approach)?

11. Discussion
    a. Are there any intervening variables invoked to "explain" the findings, i.e., what theoretical constructs are used, such as guilt, fear, etc.?
    b. Is there a simpler explanation of the results? That is, can a smaller number of explanatory concepts suffice to explain a particular finding?
    c. Are there any alternative explanations which may be less simple but more reasonable?
    d. Are there any suggestions (explicit or implicit) for future studies to resolve ambiguities in the present study or to answer questions raised by the present study?
    e. What experiments would you suggest to improve or extend the findings?

12. Conclusions

    a.   Are the conclusions drawn from the experiment justified?

    b.   What conclusions would you draw?

    c.   Are there any implications of the experiment for use as a technique in attacking practical problems?

13. Artifacts. At any appropriate point in the outline, insert notes about errors, uncontrolled events, etc. Be sure to use quotation marks when abstracting directly and give the page citation.

The Student as an Agent
of Political and
Social Reform

*ASK NOT WHAT YOUR COUNTRY IS DOING TO CHANGE YOU,
BUT WHAT YOU CAN DO TO CHANGE YOUR COUNTRY.*

"But what can *I* do to change anything?" asks the concerned citizen who perceives that social forces are determining an undesirable destiny for him. Start by trying to change the attitudes and behavior of one other person, and then another, and another. As more people who share your beliefs and values also become active agents of persuasion, the potential for basic political and social reform increases.

Central to any program of change is a statement of the goals or specific behavioral objectives, a catalogue of potentially useful techniques to implement these goals, and a means of evaluating the success of the techniques and the entire action program. We will provide one possible set of goals along with relevant questions that must be answered about resources, priorities, and related matters. A sample of techniques follows, gleaned from the available, though often inadequate, attitude-change literature, from our observation, experience, and intuition, as well as from pragmatically oriented, "naive" psychological sources such as salesmen, police interrogators, and others (discussed in Chapters 2 and 6). We conclude with a suggested approach for starting a data bank which will help evaluate the effectiveness of these persuasion techniques and establish a sounder basis for reformulating such a guide to practical persuasion.

SPECIFYING YOUR GOALS

Before embarking on your change program, the goals or consequences which you wish your program to have must be considered. In trying to decide on the goals, serious thought should be given to the following problems.

1) Begin by being specific. Even if your final goal is to change the structure of the entire established system, start out with more specific goals. The more specific your initial goals, the easier it will be to devise a technique for changing attitudes or behavior. (For example, it is not enough to want to stop environmental pollution. You must specify those sources of pollution which should be stopped first.) You must then decide who or what organization requires changing, what kind of change (behavior or attitude) is required, and how that change can be most effectively produced.

2) Almost any general goal one has can be broken down into many specific subgoals. Reaching each subgoal will make it more likely that the final goal will be attained. By dividing things into small, *highly specific* and attainable subgoals one can shape each unit of change, reinforce the people or organization who changed, and move on to the next *very specific* subgoal, until by successive approximations and reinforcement, the final goal has been attained.

3) When each subgoal is specified, try to estimate both the long-term ideological goals and the short-term tactical consequences of reaching and not reaching that goal. It is essential, in specifying a goal, to keep in mind what might happen if you fail to reach that goal. What will it mean to you? More importantly, what will the people or organization whom you are trying to influence learn about you? Always weigh the positive and negative consequences of attempting to produce a specific change, with regard to both your successes and your failures. It is almost always true that it is better to have many very small successes and no failures, than one big success and a big failure.

4) Review the questions outlined in Chapter 1. These are meant to direct your attention to a sample of the types of question one should ask oneself.

5) Compare your goals with the resources at your disposal. Try to specify tactical goals which match the resources you have. If you cannot, then make one of your first approximations or subgoals the stockpiling of appropriate resources (money, mass support, support of influential people or groups, etc.).

6) Your final consideration ought to be evaluation of the success of each change attempt. This is so important to any influence program that we are presenting this in its own section (see the penultimate section of this Postscript).

A SAMPLE OF INFLUENCE TECHNIQUES AND APPROACHES

There are many ways to organize this set of persuasive techniques (in fact, you should consult the references on police techniques, page 111, for other categorizations). Our functional organization follows four major steps which an individual must face in an interpersonal influence attempt:

1. preparing for the initial contact;

2. gaining access to and establishing the contact;

3. maintaining, intensifying, directing the interpersonal relationship; and

4. obtaining the commitment and terminating the contact.

The reader should be forewarned that there are probably no simple generalizations as to the effect of any given variable or technique on changing attitudes. Rather, the rule is that any laws of attitude change involve complex sets of interactions between a host of variables. The power of any given technique will vary with many factors associated with the source (credibility, attractiveness, power, delivery and style), the organization of the message, the nature of the arguments and appeals used, and with the characteristics of the receivers (intelligence, information level, involvement, self-esteem, sex), as well as many situational elements. Therefore, these suggested techniques should be viewed as simplistic approximations of the complex reality we are trying to understand and manipulate. Individually, they will work for some of the people some of the time. It is up to you to help develop a more adequate technology of attitude change by being aware of the many subtleties and complexities involved and carefully evaluating your hits and misses.

1. PREPARING FOR THE INITIAL CONTACT

A. *Be informed.* Get as much accurate, up-to-date, reliable evidence as you can. Commit important facts, arguments, statistics and quotations to memory so that they are "natural" to your delivery. You should see yourself as more expert on the particular issue of concern than the people you will try to persuade. Your perceived competence is your single, most important source trait.

B. *Learn as much as you can about those you will engage.* Be familiar with their neighborhood, local issues, basic values, language style (use of diction, clichés, idioms), sources of local pride and discontent, the nature of popular influence media, their attitudes on the issue in question. You can obtain this information from local businessmen (barbers, cab drivers, grocery-store employees, bartenders), from salesmen, from signatures on newspaper petitions, and from distinguishing characteristics of the neighborhood or the individual home. You can also encourage the people to verbalize their opinions by having them call in to the campus radio station, respond to telephone surveys, or come to "open campus" meetings.

C. *Actively role-play the anticipated situation with a friend.* Imagine, and then work through as realistically as possible, the persuasion situation in which you will operate. If available, tape-record or video-tape such dress rehearsals, and then critically analyze your performance. Switch roles and try to be the target person in the situation where he is experiencing the pressure to comply with a request for some commitment.

D. *Do a critical self-appraisal.* Before you actually start out, analyze your own personal strengths and weaknesses and your appearance, and verbalize any source of fear, anxiety, or anticipated embarrassment, with one or more others with whom you feel comfortable.

E. *You must be confident that you will be effective more often than not.* You must expect some setbacks, but you must be dedicated to winning, to making the "sale." If you do not handle the situation carefully, you may produce the undesirable effect of increasing the person's resistance to any further influence attempts by others; or you may generate a "boomerang" effect, causing the person to become even more extremely "con" on this position.

F. *Be sensitive to the varied reasons underlying the attitude(s) in question.* Attitudes are formed and maintained because of needs for information (cognitive clarity and consistency), for social acceptance by other people, or for ego protection from unacceptable impulses and ideas. Involving attitudes probably have all three of these motivational bases. New informational input helps in the first instance; providing new sources of reinforcement is necessary for the second; while substituting other attitudes and actions which will satisfy the same underlying ego needs must be used for the third. Information *per se* is probably the least effective way of changing attitudes and behavior. It must be part of a general approach, which sees the individual as more than a rational, information-processor—as sometimes irrational, inconsistent, responding to social rewards, and concerned about how he appears to himself and to others.

G. *Even as a stranger you can exert considerable influence.* You can serve as a model for some behavior by publicly engaging in it, and you can provide a new source of social contact, recognition, and reward for many people.

2. GAINING ACCESS TO AND ESTABLISHING THE CONTACT

A.   Before you can persuade, you must get the person to acknowledge your presence, to attend to you and to follow your presentation. People are wary of an assault on their privacy and their life space, either by a stranger thrusting a leaflet into their hand, or by an unknown person on their doorstep.

1.   In distributing materials in the street, make eye contact while the person is a short distance away, smile, and then present the leaflet at the level of his hand (as in a handshake), saying "thank you" just before they accept it. Then say, "I hope you will look it over as soon as you have time," since the person will feel awkward at either accepting it and not stopping to read it, or by being made to stop his ongoing activity unexpectedly.

2.   You might want to consider an initial phone call or letter to contacts to be made at home. However, the nature of your visit should be described in generalities which will neither threaten nor offer reasons for preparing counterarguments (e.g., "to find out your views on several important issues facing our country, such as ecology, education, and the war").

B.   If you are making a home contact, be aware of the particular situation you have encountered. Be sure that the person is willing to give you the required time to present your case. You might be interrupting dinner, a phone call, a family quarrel, a visit with guests, or some bad news. You do not want the dominant motivation of the homeowner to be to get rid of you as soon as possible.

C.   Where possible, it is advisable to select a contact situation where you and the target person are either equals (you are a "guest" in the home only as long as the host allows it), or you have some power advantage. This occurs where you are buying merchandise, paying for a service, or where the person is dependent upon you for your services.

D.   Those people known or expected to be against your position should be contacted not in their familiar surroundings, but ideally on your ground. This both becomes the first act of yielding (as the police manuals tell us), and allows you greater confidence and situational control. You can then arrange a modelling situation in which a prestigious model engages in the desired goal behavior before the target person.

E.   Although strangers can influence everyday behavior, persuasion is enhanced when the target perceives some basic similarity with the source. This "strategy of identification" (practiced by all good entertainers and politicians) involves finding some commonality between you. Physical similarity is the most obvious; age, sex, race, ethnic features, dress (distribution of hair), voice dialect, regionalisms, and appropriate slang, jargon, or group-identifying phrases (e.g., "What can you expect from the Goyim?", "If the market bottoms out at 550, then what do you think will happen?").

Canvassing should be arranged to optimize this perceived similarity by selecting neighborhoods and locations which are approximately matched to the available canvassers. The canvasser should try to uncover as many points of similarity as possible because similarity breeds familiarity, which promotes liking and enhances credibility and greater acceptance of the message.

F. Similarity may be created and combined with an "overheard communication" approach, as in the following example: A young coed enters a laundromat with a basket of laundry, puts it in the machine, asks another customer for change of a quarter to make a phone call to her mother, pretends to call Mom, describes the chores she is and will be doing ("She's a good daughter"), then may proceed to talk to her mother briefly about the attitude topic and agree with her mother's course of action. She talks loudly enough to let the target audience hear, but goes about her business when she is finished, unless one of them initiates the conversation.

G. Students are not seen as credible. sources on most issues that concern them directly; to be effective, it is important to increase source credibility. This may be accomplished in a number of ways:

1. Impress the audience with your expertise, concern, and dedication, being forceful but not overbearing.

2. Argue on some points which are against your own best interests; indicate the sacrifices you have made and would be willing to make.

3. Have a respected person introduce you, or make the contact for you.

4. Begin by agreeing with what the audience wants to hear, or a "pro-them" approach (the Mark Antony effect).

5. Minimize your manipulative intent until you ask for the commitment.

H. The potential for persuasion in general is greater among women than among men; also it is greater if the message is delivered in a situation where there is positive affect serving as a minimal distractor; and if small compliances (like agreeing to talk to you for ten minutes) precede the escalation to more extreme ones (the "foot-in-the-door technique").

I. People are more likely to comply with the request of a person who has some stigma (an eye patch, or a cane, for example) if compliance does not involve any further personal contact. Stutterers are likely to be very effective in securing behavioral compliance (e.g., letter-writing or telephoning) since they will be seen as willing to expose their handicap for their beliefs, and also because the target person will feel awkward and be eager to terminate the interaction as quickly as possible. Guilt for feeling so may motivate compliance.

J. Avoid group situations where the majority are known or expected to be against you, since they will provide support for each other and make salient a group norm under attack.

3. MAINTAINING, INTENSIFYING, DIRECTING
THE INTERPERSONAL RELATIONSHIP

Once you have managed to get the person to listen to you, you must hold this attention, while trying to get your message (and yourself) accepted.

A. You have the power to reinforce many behaviors of the target person—a power you should use judiciously but with conscious awareness of what and how you are reinforcing.

1. Attentive listening to what the other person has to say about anything of personal interest is absolutely necessary. This not only "opens up" the person for a dialogue, and helps in establishing what are the primary values, the beliefs, and the organization of his (or her) thinking, but it establishes you as someone open to what others have to say. (The opportunity to tell a college student where to get off may be very rewarding for many people.)

2. Use eye contact with the person as a reward when the target person says something with which you agree. Always maintain as close physical proximity as seems acceptable.

3. Individuate the person by using names (with Mr. or Mrs. or titles, when there is an age or status discrepancy). Make the person feel you are reacting to his uniqueness and individuality (which you should be) and are not reacting in a programmed way to your stereotyped conception of a housewife, blue-collar worker, etc. Similarly, help the other person to individuate you, to break through the categorization and pigeon-holing process which makes you just an anonymous canvasser. At some point, describe something personal or unique about your feelings, background, or interests (which you expect will be acceptable). However, once this is accomplished, don't allow yourself to be the exception to the stereotype—say "most other students are like me in how we feel about X."

4. Reinforce specific behaviors explicitly and immediately, by nodding, saying "Good," "That's an interesting point," etc. Reinforce more general classes of behavior by smiling, by making it obvious you enjoy the interaction, and by being impressed by the person's openness, sensitivity, intelligence, or articulateness. As a college student with much "book learning" you can still learn a lot from people who have gone to "the school of hard knocks", and who have "real-life learning," and "street savvy" to offer you. Let them know that's how you feel when talking to someone who has not had the benefit of a college education.

5. The person must perceive that you personally care about and are enthusiastic about the item(s) under discussion; moreover, you must be perceived as really caring about the compliant act of the person—at a personal level and not merely as part of your role.

6. Your reinforcement rate should increase over the course of the interaction, so that at the end of the time the person is sorry to see you leave.

B.   Be aware of the sources of resentment against you for what you represent by your physical appearance, group membership (as a student), etc.; work to differentiate those feelings and reactions from the goal of your influence attempt.

C.   Plan the organization of your presentation well enough so that it seems natural and unplanned, and be *flexible* enough to modify it as necessary.

1.   Do not put your best arguments in the middle of your presentation where they are least well remembered. Put your strongest arguments first if you want to motivate or interest uninvolved people; use a climax order with people whose interest is already high.

2.   Draw your conclusions explicitly. Implicit conclusion drawing should be left for only very intelligent audiences.

3.   Repeat the main points in your argument, and the major points of agreement between you and the target person.

D.   In tailoring your approach to the target person:

1.   Do not put him on the defensive, or even encourage or force a public defense of (and thus commitment to) his "con-you" position. Opposing beliefs are to be seen as providing the opportunity for open discussion, as a starting point to find areas of common agreement. If the person is "pro-you," then *do* get a public commitment early, and try to make it more stable and more extreme by applying reinforcements appropriately.

2.   Get the person to role-play your position or one which he does not agree with (if the situation allows it).

3.   Have the person restate your ideas and conclusions for himself, in his own words (encourage active participation, especially if participation is "pro-you").

4.   If the person appears to be very authoritarian in manner and thinking, then he will probably be more impressed by status sources, and appeals to power, control, decisiveness, and one-sided generalizations than by informational appeals, expert testimony, unbiased presentation of both sides of the issue, etc. Any approach must be responsive to the dominant personality and social characteristics of the person to whom you are talking.

5.   Play the devil's advocate for a "pro-you" person in order to get him to defend his position, to articulate it clearly, to practice handling counter-arguments, and to be reinforced for doing so, by your "coming around to agree with him."

6.   For the "con-you" person, the "reactance technique" (see page 118) may be effective. You limit his sense of psychological freedom by stating a very extreme position, one with which he could not entirely agree, prefacing it with, "*no one* could disagree with the statement that . . .," or "you *must*

acknowledge that . . .," or *"everybody* is convinced that . . .". It is expected that the response will be, *"I* don't agree," and then you reinforce his overt statement of disagreement with positions on the "other side" of the issue. For such a person, the goal of the interaction may be to instill doubt in his former set of beliefs, or force a wedge between some apparently inseparable cognitive links. In this way, the person might become more receptive to subsequent persuasion by the mass media or through exposure to new events.

7.   Although a more personal relationship can be established in a two-person interaction, there is much to be gained from team work. Working in pairs provides each student with social support, lowers apprehension about initiating each new contact, allows one of you to be "off the firing line" and appraising the situation, to come in when help is needed, to refocus the direction, or to respond to some specific trait detected in the target person. The third party also permits a better evaluation of the dynamics of the interaction after it is terminated. Teamwork can be used to tactical advantage, as the police recommend with the "Mutt and Jeff" technique (see page 113), modified as the "militant and the moderate." In addition, a consistent, agreeing minority of two individuals who are perceived as strangers (or at least not in collusion) has been shown to be effective in modifying the attitudes of a majority. This may be even more so when the minority disagree on other issues, but totally agree on this one.

4. GETTING THE COMMITMENT AND TERMINATING THE CONTACT

You must now get what you came for; don't insist that the person accept and believe what you've said before he makes the behavioral commitment. Get the behavioral commitment anyway, and attitude change will follow. The ideal conclusion of the contact would also leave the person feeling that the time spent was worthwhile and his self-esteem is higher than it was before you arrived.

A. Do not overstay your welcome, or be forced to stay longer than is worthwhile according to your time schedule. Timing is essential both in knowing when to ask for the commitment, and in knowing when to quit with an intractable person. For a person who needs more time to think, encourage it, but get a commitment to allow you to come back.

B. You might provide several behavioral alternatives for the person, arranged in degrees of difficulty. *After* getting commitment on the easy alternatives, push for the more difficult ones.

C.   Be clear as to what actions are requested, or what has been agreed on or concluded. If fear appeals have been used, then solutions must be offered which are clear, explicit, and involve a concrete course of action to alleviate the danger.

D.   A "bandwagon" effect may be used to indicate prestigious others who have joined in the action.

E.   When you believe the target person is about to make the commitment (or after a verbal agreement is made), then stress the fact that the decision is his own; it involves free choice and no pressure. At the same time, minimize extrinsic sources of justification for the discrepant compliance. By creating dissonance (see Chapter 5) at this point, you impel the individual to make his behavior internally consistent by generating his own intrinsic justifications for his behavior. But afterwards, reinforce the person's behavior with thanks and appreciation.

F.   Emotionally inoculate the person from counterattacks by noting that there will be people who will disagree with his action by saying "A, B, and C." How will he respond to such critics?

G.   Broaden the contact in three ways. First, get the name of one or more neighbors who would agree with the person's position. You will talk to them, too, and use the person's name if that is okay with him. Secondly, see if the person will go out and proselytize his friends and relatives to further support the action taken. This extends your influence and is the *best* commitment from the person. Finally, honestly react to something about the person which is irrelevant to the main social/political issue at hand: the house, decor, hair, clothes, an avocation mentioned, or a favor which you can do related to something mentioned.

H.   Finally, indicate there is a possibility for future contact (for "surveillance" of the commitment), and that you would like to talk again about other things. Perhaps you could call again or be called (leave your name and number).

I.   Thank the person for his (or her) time and the interesting dialogue. For those who made the commitment, emphasize how much better things would be if there were more such people. For the recalcitrant person, say you'll think about all of the things he has said, *if* he does the same about what you said.

J.   Before going to the next interaction, stop and think about what you have learned about yourself and about human nature, where you were effective, and where you went wrong. Think about (or complete) an evaluation of this interaction.

EVALUATION OF THE CHANGE PROGRAM

One of the most important aspects of any activity whose goal is to produce a change in the behavior or attitudes of people is evaluation of the effectiveness of that activity in producing the hoped-for change. Evaluation is important for a number of reasons. First, many of the techniques you have just read about have not been tested in field settings, and therefore, some of them may not work. Second, some techniques may be more effective than others, and without an evaluation of the relative effectiveness of each of the techniques you will not know whether you are using the most effective technique possible. Third, shaping (see the section on specifying goals) can only work if you know when each subgoal has been reached; the next goal in the series should not be attempted until each previous subgoal has been achieved. Fourth, information which you obtain about the effectiveness of various techniques can be used by others who have the same goals as you do. This will prevent the repetition of mistakes (see Chapter 5 on symbolic modelling). Avoiding the repetition of mistakes will greatly increase the long-term effectiveness of any organized change program.

To aid you in devising a method of evaluation, a sample of the types of objective data you might want to gather daily is outlined below.

A Format for Evaluating Your Persuasion Attempt

I. The change agent (you)

    A. Physical characteristics

        1. Sex
        2. Age
        3. Dress
        4. Race/ethnic background
        5. Unusual physical characteristics (i.e., eye patch, broken leg, etc.)
        6. Other thought to be relevant

    B. Psychological characteristics

        1. Educational level
        2. Socioeconomic background
        3. Interpersonal contact made alone or with _____ others (how many?)
        4. Familiarity with change techniques employed

5. Dominant personality features (forceful, serious, shy, sincere, etc.)
6. Other

II. The target person (or group)

   A. Physical characteristics (same as above)

   B. Psychological characteristics

      1. Same as above plus those below.

      2. History of attitude or behavior which is to be changed

         a) Does the person initially agree or disagree with you?

         b) Has the person acted either in favor of or in opposition to goal in the past?

         c) Have others tried to change the person (failed or succeeded)?

         d) If yes to former question, what techniques were employed?

      3. Influence of target person

         a) Does person have control of many useful resources other than his vote or attitude? (Assess spread of potential influence.)

         b) Will person have time to work for/with you to change others?

III. Situation in which contact is made

   A. Place (home of target person or other)

   B. Time of day: Activity which target person was engaged in immediately before contact

   C. Duration of contact

   D. Your role

   E. Target person's role

   F. Other relevant events which occurred during contact

IV. What was your goal for this contact (be specific!)?

V. What technique(s) was (were) employed to reach that goal?

VI. To what degree was your goal achieved?

VII. On what *objective, behavioral* data do you base this answer?

VIII. What other evidence might you have gathered? (Describe)

IX. What factors do you feel produced the final result for this contact (with regard to you, the target person, the situation, the technique, the goal)?

X. Any other general comments which might affect future attempts.

CONCLUDING STATEMENT

Any student who plans to go out into the "real world" to try to influence others, to change attitudes, and to modify behavior must be aware of the personal as well as the social consequences of such a decision:

> The psychologist can hardly do anything without realizing that for him the acquisition of knowledge opens up the most terrifying prospects of controlling what people do and how they think and how they behave and how they feel.

J. Robert Oppenheimer

References

References

Abelson, H. I. and Karlins, M. *Persuasion: How Opinions and Attitudes Are Changed.* New York: Springer, 1959. Revised edition in preparation.

Allyn, J. and Festinger, L. The effectiveness of unanticipated persuasion communications. *J. abn. soc. Psychol.,* 1961, **62,** 35-40.

Anderson, K. E. and Clevenger, T. A summary of experimental research in Ethos. *Speech Monographs,* 1963, **30,** 59-78.

Aronson, E. and Mills, J. The effect of severity of initiation on liking for a group. *J. abn. soc. Psychol.,* 1959, **59,** 177-181.

Bandura, A., Blanchard, E. D., and Ritter, B. J. The relative efficacy of desensitization and modeling therapeutic approaches for inducing behavioral, affective and attitudinal changes. Unpublished manuscript, Stanford University, 1968.

Bandura, A. and Walters, R. H. *Social Learning and Personality Development.* New York: Holt, Rinehart, and Winston, 1963.

Bem, D. Inducing beliefs in false confessions. *J. pers. soc. Psychol.,* 1966, **3,** 707-710.

Bem, D. Self-perception: An alternative interpretation of cognitive dissonance phenomena. *Psychol. Rev.,* 1967, **74,** 183-200.

Brehm, J. W. *A Theory of Psychological Reactance.* New York: Academic Press, 1966.

Cameron, P., Frank, F., Lifter, M., and Morrissey, P. Cognitive functionings of college students in a general psychology class. Paper presented at a meeting of the American Psychological Association, 1968.

Campbell, D. T. and Stanley, J. C. *Experimental and Quasi-experimental Designs for Research.* Chicago: Rand McNally, 1963.

Cohen, A. R. Communication discrepancy and attitude change: A dissonance theory approach. *J. Pers.*, 1959, **27**, 386-396.

Cohen, A. R. A "forced compliance" experiment on repeated dissonances. In J. W. Brehm and A. R. Cohen, *Explorations in Cognitive Dissonance*. New York: Wiley, 1962, pp. 97-104.

Cohen, A. R., Greenbaum, C. W., and Mansson, H. H. Commitment to social deprivation and verbal conditioning. *J. abn. soc. Psychol.*, 1963, **67**, 410-422.

Conant, J. B. *On Understanding Science*. New Haven: Yale University Press, 1951.

Crowne, D. P. and Marlowe, D. *The Approval Motive*. New York: Wiley, 1964.

Dichter, E. *Handbook of Consumer Motivations*. New York: McGraw-Hill, 1964.

Ehrlich, P. R. *The Population Bomb*. New York: Ballantine Books, 1968.

Ellsworth, P. C. and Carlsmith, J. M. Effects of eye contact and verbal content on affective response to a dyadic interaction. *J. pers. soc. Psychol.*, 1968, **10**, 15-20.

Ewing, T. A study of certain factors involved in the study of changes of opinion. *J. soc. Psychol.*, 1942, **16**, 63-88.

Festinger, L. *A Theory of Cognitive Dissonance*. Evanston, Illinois: Row, Peterson, 1957.

Festinger, L. and Carlsmith, J. M. Cognitive consequences of forced compliance. *J. abn. soc. Psychol.*, 1959, **58**, 203-211.

Festinger, L. and Maccoby, N. On resistance to persuasive communications. *J. abn. soc. Psychol.*, 1964, **68**, 359-366.

Freedman, J. L. and Fraser, S. C. Compliance without pressure: The foot-in-the-door technique. *J. pers. soc. Psychol.*, 1966, **4**, 195-202.

Freedman, J. L. and Sears, D. O. Warning, distraction and resistance to influence. *J. pers. soc. Psychol.*, 1965, **1**, 262-266.

Frenkel-Brunswick, E., Levinson, D. J., and Sanford, R. N. The anti-democratic personality. In E. E. Maccoby, T. M. Newcomb, E. L. Hartley (eds.), *Readings in Social Psychology*. New York: Holt, Rinehart, Winston, 1958, pp. 636-646.

Gerard, H. B. and Mathewson, G. C. The effects of severity of initiation on liking for a group: A replication. *J. exp. soc. Psychol.*, 1966, **2**, 278-287.

Giffin, K. The contribution of studies of source credibility to a theory of interpersonal trust in the communication process. *Psychol. Bull.*, 1967, **68**, 104-120.

Hammond, E. C. Smoking and death rates—a riddle in cause and effect. *Amer. Scientist*, 1958, **46**, 331-354.

Hitler, A. *Mein Kampf.* Trans. by E. T. S. Dugdale. Cambridge, Massachusetts: Riverside Press, 1933.

Hovland, C. I. Reconciling conflicting results derived from experimental and survey studies of attitude change. *Amer. Psychologist,* 1959, **14**, 8-17.

Hovland, C. I., Harvey, O. J., and Sherif, M. Assimilation and contrast effects in reaction to communication and attitude change. *J. abn. soc. Psychol.,* 1957, **55**, 244-252.

Hovland, C. I., Janis, I. L., and Kelley, H. H. *Communication and Persuasion.* New Haven: Yale University Press, 1953.

Hovland, C. I., Lumsdaine, A. A., and Sheffield, F. D. *Experiments on mass communication.* Vol. III of *Studies in Social Psychology in World War II.* Princeton: Princeton University Press, 1949.

Hovland, C. I. and Weiss, W. The influence of source credibility on communication effectiveness. *Publ. Opin. Quart.,* 1951, **15**, 635-650.

Inbau, F. E. and Reid, J. E. *Lie Detection and Criminal Interrogation.* Baltimore: Williams and Wilkins, 1953.

Inbau, F. E. and Reid, J. E. *Criminal Interrogation and Confessions.* Baltimore: Williams and Wilkins, 1962.

Insko, C. I. *Theories of Attitude Change.* New York: Appleton-Century-Crofts, 1967.

Janis, I. L. and Feshbach, S. Effects of fear-arousing communications. *J. abn. soc. Psychol.,* 1953, **48**, 78-92.

Janis, I. L. and King, B. T. The influence of role-playing on opinion change. *J. abn. soc. Psychol.,* 1954, **49**, 211-218.

Jansen, M. J. and Stolurow, L. M. An experimental study of role playing. *Psychol. Monogr.,* 1962, **76**, No. 31.

Katz, D. The functional approach to the study of attitudes. *Publ. Opin. Quart.,* 1960, **24**, 163-204.

Katz, E. and Lazarsfeld, P. F. *Personal Influence.* Glencoe, Ill.: The Free Press, 1955.

Kidd, W. R. Police interrogation. *The Police Journal.* New York, 1940.

Kiesler, C. A., Collins, B. E., and Miller, N. *Attitude Change: A Critical Analysis of Theoretical Approaches.* New York: Wiley, 1969.

Kiesler, C. A. and Kiesler, S. B. *Conformity.* Reading, Massachusetts: Addison-Wesley, 1969.

King, B. T. and Janis, I. L. Comparison of the effectiveness of improvised versus non-improvised role playing in producing opinion changes. *Hum. Relat.,* 1956, **9**, 177-186.

Lewin, K., Lippitt, R., and White, R. K. Patterns of aggressive behavior in experimentally oriented "social climates." *J. soc. Psychol.,* 1939, **10**, 271-299.

McGuire, W. J. The nature of attitudes and attitude change. In G. Lindzey and E. Aronson (eds.), *Handbook of Social Psychology*. Reading, Mass.: Addison-Wesley, 1969. Vol. III, 136-314.

McGuire, W. J. and Papageorgis, D. Effectiveness of forewarning in developing resistance to persuasion. *Publ. Opin. Quart.*, 1962, **26**, 24-34.

Miller, N. and Baron, R. Communicator credibility as a mediator of "distraction" effects in studies of persuasion. Unpublished manuscript, University of Minnesota, 1968.

Miller, N. and Campbell, D. T. Recency and primacy in persuasion as a function of the timing of speeches and measurements. *J. abn. soc. Psychol.*, 1959, **59**, 1-9.

Mischel, W. *Personality Assessment*. New York: Wiley, 1968.

Mulbar, H. *Interrogation*. Springfield, Ill.: Thomas, 1951.

Nizer, L. *My Life in Court*. New York: Pyramid, 1961.

O'Hara, C. E. *Fundamentals of Criminal Investigation*. Springfield, Ill.: Thomas, 1956.

Packard, V. O. *The Hidden Persuaders*. New York: McKay, 1957.

Paul, G. *Insight vs. Desensitization in Psychotherapy*. Stanford: Stanford University Press, 1965.

Qualter, T. H. *Propaganda and Psychological Warfare*. New York: Random House, 1962.

Rowland, M. and Young, L. Survey of sexual behavior at Stanford. Unpublished manuscript, Stanford University, November 1968.

Sarnoff, I. Psychoanalytic theory and social attitudes. *Publ. Opin. Quart.*, 1960, **24**, 251-279.

Smith, E. E. Methods for changing consumer attitudes: A report of three experiments. Project Report. Quartermaster Food and Container Institute for the Armed Forces (PRA Report 61-2). February 1961a. (See Smith, 1961b)

Smith, E. E. The power of dissonance techniques to change attitudes. *Publ. Opin. Quart.*, 1961b, **25**, 626-639.

Stouffer, S. A., Suchman, E. A., DeVinney, L. C., Star, S. A., and Williams, R. M., Jr. *The American Soldier: Adjustments during Army Life*. Vol. I of *Studies in Social Psychology in World War II*. Princeton: Princeton University Press, 1949.

Tresselt, M. E. The effect of the experience of contrasted groups upon the formation of a new scale of judgment. *J. soc. Psychol.*, 1948, **27**, 209-216.

Zimbardo, P. G., Ebbesen, E. B., and Fraser, S. C. Emotional persuasion: Arousal state as a distractor. Unpublished manuscript, Stanford University, 1968.

Zimbardo, P. G., Weisenberg, M., Firestone, I., and Levy, B. Communicator effectiveness in producing public conformity and private attitude change. *J. Pers.*, 1965, **33**, 233-256.